AN INTRODUCTORY COMPOSITION COURSE FOR STUDENTS OF ENGLISH

Beverly Ingram
Carol King

CAMBRIDGE UNIVERSITY PRESS

Published by the Press Syndicate of the University of Cambridge
The Pitt Building, Trumpington Street, Cambridge CB2 1RP
40 West 20th Street, New York, NY 10011-4211, USA
10 Stamford Road, Oakleigh, Melbourne 3166, Australia

First published 1988
Ninth printing 1996

Printed in the United States of America

Library of Congess Cataloging-in-Publication Data
Ingram, Beverly, 1949-
From writing to composing : an introductory composition course
for students of English / Beverly Ingram, Carol King.
p.   cm.
"Student's book"
ISBN 0-521-37938-5
1. English language – Textbooks for foreign speakers. 2. English
language – Composition and exercises.   I. King, Carol, 1947-
II. Title.
PE1128.I477   1988b
808'.042–dc19   88–25723
                                                            CIP

ISBN 0-521-37938-5 Student's Book
ISBN 0-521-37939-3 Teacher's Manual

Book design by Peter Ducker

Contents

Unit 4   Describing places   66

Unit 5   Describing people   82

Unit 6   Describing people's lives   103

Appendixes   168

Acknowledgments

We want to express our appreciation to the students, faculty, and administration of The English Language Center at LaGuardia Community College of the City University of New York, the Intensive English Program of the University of Texas at Austin, and the Intensive English Program of the Texas International Education Consortium in the College of Preparatory Studies of the Institut Teknologi MARA in Malaysia. In particular, we would like to thank Linda Austin, Ray Cowart, Gloria Gallingane, Lynn Giudici, Jim Hawkins, Mary Kracklauer, Suma Kurien, Carol Odell, and Kathy Schmitz as well as other teachers too numerous to mention who used early drafts of the materials and made useful suggestions for improving them. We also owe special thanks to Colleen O'Connell and David Moreno, who generously donated their time and energy in creating original artwork for the pilot edition which, though it does not appear here, was an invaluable contribution. And, because their presence is felt on page after page of this book, we want to thank numerous other colleagues in many places for their important contributions to our professional growth and development over the years. We also want to give some personal thank-you's. Carol thanks her mother, Edith King, whose constant love and support have given her the confidence to tackle anything. Beverly thanks her husband, Phillip Sladek, and her parents, Gwen and Truitt Ingram, for their warm, unwavering support through the years and for countless hours of babysitting during this project. Finally, Carol and Bev thank each other for the long friendship and shared experiences that made this book a reality.

The authors and publisher are grateful to the following for permission to reproduce illustrations and photographs: Steve Delmonte (pp. 4, 36, 126 except bottom right, 127 except top left, 128 top left and bottom right); Tom Ickert (pp. 11, 16, 20, 21, 22, 23, 26, 33, 34, 43, 45, 46, 56, 60, 61, 69, 72, 83, 84, 85, 95, 97, 105, 106, 113); Elivia Savadier-Sagov (pp. 78, 126 bottom right, 127 top left, 128 bottom left and top right); J & R Art Services (pp. 67, 71, 94); John F. Kennedy Library (pp. 28, 29); Edward Starr Collection, Department of Special Collections, Mugar Memorial Library, Boston University Libraries (p. 40 top left); Donald S. Pitkin (p. 40 bottom left); The Yomiuri Shimbun, Tokyo (p. 40 top right); Southwest Museum, Los Angeles (p. 40 bottom right); U.S. Department of the Interior, National Park Service, Edison National Historic Site (pp. 53, 90, 105); UPI/Bettmann (p. 103).

Cover design by Dennis M. Arnold
Book design by Peter Ducker

To the Teacher

What is *From Writing to Composing* all about?

From Writing to Composing is a composition textbook for beginning and low-intermediate ESL/EFL students. Through activities ranging from structured "writing" to free "composing," students will become more fluent and confident writers of general-purpose English. Teachers and students can select from a variety of lighthearted and serious topics and activities. Related listening-speaking tasks develop vocabulary, reinforce sound-symbol relationships, and contribute to a lively, motivating classroom atmosphere.

A comprehensive Teacher's Manual, available separately, contains essential materials that do not appear in the Student's Book. It also shows the teacher how to guide students through simple revision and editing of their compositions. Both Student's Book and Teacher's Manual offer many ways for students to interact through their writing and about their writing. Two long-range projects, the Class Newspaper Project and the Family History Project, provide a sustained audience, purpose, and outlet for student work.

From Writing to Composing has been field tested in large and small classes worldwide. It is intended for classroom use in intensive, semi-intensive, adult education, university, and secondary school courses.

What does the title *From Writing to Composing* mean?

The title refers to the way we approach teaching composition to lower-level students and the way we have organized the book. Each unit in the book develops one or more topics by moving students from structured "writing" activities to free "composing" activities. Here are the basic differences between these two distinctly different types of activities:

1. A composition is rarely, if ever, finished in one work session, whereas a writing assignment is usually completed on the first try.
2. With composing activities, the teacher should generally ignore, and similarly encourage students to disregard, surface-level problems in grammar and mechanics until the content has been reworked several times and is ready for editing. With writing activities, however, the teacher should expect students to pay close attention to such details and correct the assignments the first and probably only time they are turned in.
3. Composing has a purpose beyond learning the language and an audience other than or in addition to the teacher. A writing assignment, on the other hand, is done only to practice English and only for the teacher's scrutiny.
4. A good composition deserves to be shown off in the class newspaper or on the classroom wall; a writing assignment probably does not.

Because they serve different purposes, "writing" activities and "composing" activities are equally important in a lower-level composition course. Because lower-level students have relatively little language at their disposal, they need a variety of structured writing activities that will give them something to say about a given topic and the language to say it with before confronting a composition assignment on the same topic. Then, after students have put their basic ideas down on paper, they need composing activities that will guide them through the process of rereading, rewriting, revising, and correcting their work until the final compositions communicate their ideas as clearly and accurately as possible. The Teacher's Manual has these activities.

Why are listening and speaking activities included?

Although the primary purpose of the book is to elicit a great deal of structured and free written work, a strong oral component is essential for lower-level students because they still need basic vocabulary on many common topics. Without oral work, many students would end up doing the structured activities intended to introduce key concepts and vocabulary by merely shuffling around on paper words they had never heard and could not pronounce. When it came time for the students to begin composing, these key words would still not be part of their active vocabulary, and they would be unable to handle the assignment.

Oral activities are also important because of the value lower-level students place on developing conversation skills and because such oral work helps some students overcome their fear of writing. As they talk through an activity, these students often gain confidence to face and eventually conquer their fear of pencil and paper. (At this proficiency level we recommend that students write and compose in pencil, so they can make changes and corrections with ease.)

Why is the Teacher's Manual so important? Don't the activities in the Student's Book speak for themselves?

Lower-level students do not profit from detailed passages about drafting, revising, and editing since they are as yet unable to understand such material. They can, however, begin learning these skills through demonstration by the teacher. Thus, *From Writing to Composing* is designed so that the Teacher's Manual, not the Student's Book, shows you how to teach the composing process. While activities in the Student's Book lead students *to* composing, procedures outlined in the Teacher's Manual actually lead them *through* it. So, if you do not have the Teacher's Manual, you and your students have only half of *From Writing to Composing*.

The Teacher's Manual also furnishes exercises, activities, and ideas that change the book into a course – in short, things that it usually takes a teacher a lot of time to devise. The Teacher's Manual, then, is meant to save you time.

Should I do the activities in each unit in order, and should I finish one unit completely before beginning another?

The answer to both questions is no. Do *not* take students straight through a unit in order from start to finish. Instead, look over an *entire* unit before planning or teaching even one class session from it. Each unit is composed of several groups of activities, called "sections," which are to be interwoven and overlapped with each other and with activities from the unit that follows. Usually, on any given day in the course, you should have students working on activities from three, four, or five different sections. For example, on a given day, your class might be ready for (1) a follow-up activity on one practice text, (2) a preview activity on another practice text, (3) the first draft of one composition, (4) the editing of another composition, and (5) an Active Vocabulary Practice exercise from the following unit. Whether you could actually undertake this many activities on one day would, however, depend on the length of your class session and the mood and capabilities of your students.

Ideally, you should spend 10 to 15 hours of class time on each unit and finish the book in 12 to 15 weeks. If you have less time, you certainly don't have to cover everything in a unit. You should, however, try to do at least part of every unit. Although the units do become more difficult, some sections, such as the class trip (Unit 4), the survey about the typical student (Unit 5), and the personality profile (Unit 6), should be done at your convenience and not according to their order of appearance in the book. Some activities, particularly the Class Newspaper Project and the Family History Project, once begun should be completed even if that means omitting the rest of the unit.

How can I have my class do a newspaper? I know nothing about journalism.

Neither do we. Journalistic training is not necessary, and producing a professional product is not the point. The goal is to give students a reason to try to write well, a purpose for interacting, and a showcase for their finished work. Although access to a typewriter and photocopy or ditto machine would be handy, you can certainly handle the project quite well without either. Appendix 1 tells you how.

What exactly is the Family History Project?

In the Family History Project each student develops a biographical composition about a family member from the past to preserve for a family member in the future. In each unit, starting with Unit 2, students write, revise, and save paragraphs on given aspects of the past family member's life to integrate in Unit 6 into a composition of lasting value. The project, though challenging, will capture the imagination of your students and give them experience, even at a low level, with the kind of collecting and shaping of material that will be required of them in academic settings.

How should I decide what to do in class and what to assign for homework?

For best results with *From Writing to Composing*, do most composing work in class and as often as possible write along with the students. Spending time *in* class on composing emphasizes its importance, as does your participation as an individual. Both practices send the message that composing is something worth doing. In class, students can't easily ignore or avoid doing composition work, especially when everyone around them, including the teacher, is doing it. When students compose in class, you can observe and intervene in their writing process. When you write, the students can observe your writing process. You should not, however, feel pressure to set an example to be followed. The point to communicate is that even for the teacher, whose proficiency in English is far beyond that of the students, composing requires time, thought, and patience. Even the teacher chews the pencil, stares into space, wads up the paper, and starts again.

For homework, students should routinely produce a half page or so of text in English, principally through structured activities such as those that accompany dictation passages, practice texts, and picture compositions. This controlled type of homework takes relatively little time, so students are more likely to do it. A student who would not go home and write a composition based on a class discussion *will* go home and rewrite a practice text previewed in class. The persistent practice pays off in both expanded vocabulary and improved physical writing fluency. Furthermore, this type of homework is easy for the teacher to mark. By correcting and returning it quickly, you further encourage students to work outside class.

How can I keep the class running smoothly if I have students write in class and they finish at different times?

Since you cannot change the rate at which students write, simply expect that some people will finish ahead of others, and plan what we call "buffer work" to occupy the fast finishers until the class as a whole is ready for the next activity. It is helpful to keep a running list and small file of constructive and rather short activities to serve as buffer work. The Teacher's Manual contains many suggestions. You can have fast finishers complete a homework assignment that you have already begun in class through oral activities. You can also have them do review work by writing previously unassigned variations of structured writing activities. To keep them from perceiving such work as tedious or punitive, however, keep some activities on hand that will seem like a treat or a reward. You might, for example, have students draw classroom display copies of picture cues that you will need in Units 3 and 5. Or, provide a tape player and some taped material in an out-of-the-way corner for students to transcribe, discuss, answer questions about, or react to in some other way. Another way to make buffer work seem appealing is to save copies of especially good papers and have authors recopy them on ditto mats for the whole class. Naturally, as the course progresses, individual conferences about the revision and editing of various works-in-progress are an even better way to fill this time.

How is grammar handled?

From Writing to Composing is not a grammar book. The structured writing activities do not lead students through a progression of grammar points. Students encounter, simultaneously rather than sequentially, these four tenses: the simple present, the present continuous, the simple past, and occasionally the present perfect. The greatest emphasis is, however, on the simple past. Students are expected to gain control of tenses as well as a miscellany of other grammar points through repeated exposure and practice in a variety of writing and composing activities rather than through explicit grammar lessons.

To make the best use of this book, you must be careful in early units not to get sidetracked by the horrendous and frequent grammar mistakes your students will make in their compositions. Although brief explanations of specific grammar points are indeed necessary at times, resist the temptation to take off several days in a row from teaching composition in order to do a thorough grammar review. Instead, move on to new writing and composing activities. The constant flow of new topics will keep students' attention focused on the real goal, communicating meaning, while providing fresh opportunities to practice troublesome grammar points again and again.

My classes have 35 to 40 students. How can I use *From Writing to Composing*?

The activities in this book have been used with classes of all sizes. They worked well. Naturally, how they are managed with a large class is somewhat different than with a small one. (1) A basic recommendation regarding the structured work, which makes up the bulk of the homework, is to check a lot of it orally in class. To keep students on their toes and doing their homework on a daily basis, however, collect and grade everyone's work periodically and without warning. Or, set up a "secret" system for collecting and checking the work of only one-third or one-fourth of the class on any given day. (2) With composing work, always collect and read (but do not mark) everyone's first draft. This is quick to do and will give you an overview of each person's problems and help you select activities useful to everyone. You will of course have to spend considerable time, on a frequent basis, editing and reacting to each person's almost-final and final compositions. (3) With both writing and composing activities, use pair and group work to the maximum to ensure that each person gets a lot of individual interaction time in each class session. (4) To make sure that *you* stay in touch with each person on a regular basis, have students interact with you, and practice their writing skills at the same time, by writing in a dialog journal and turning it in for your reaction on a regular basis. (5) Finally, get and use the Teacher's Manual. It is extensive and specific. It will free you from detailed, time-consuming lesson planning and allow you time outside of class to give your student's work the attention it deserves.

Should I have my students buy spirals or looseleaf notebooks for their written work?

We strongly recommend a looseleaf notebook with dividers. Students can file handouts along with their papers in a looseleaf notebook and organize related items together. Dividers are useful because several activities in *From Writing to Composing* require students to retrieve particular papers done in previous units. Also, as the notebook grows in thickness, it serves as a tangible marker of progress that gives a sense of accomplishment, even if it is only thrown away at the end of the course. Furthermore, students' compositions are simply not acceptable in any setting if written on ragged-edged paper torn from a spiral, and if compositions are left in a spiral, it is not easy to exchange or display them. For everyone's efficiency and economy, it is a good idea to coordinate the notebook with the students' other skill-area teachers. Specify enough dividers to make sections for filing students' papers and handouts from all courses, not just those from the composition course.

From Writing to Composing

Unit 1   Getting Started

(see Teacher's Manual pp. 1–14)

1.1   LETTERS ABOUT PEOPLE: Practice text

Activity A: Interviewing a classmate

1. Write questions to get these facts about a classmate. Work with your class.

2. Work with a partner. Ask your partner the questions. Write the answers on a piece of paper.

3. Introduce your partner to the class. Tell the class about your partner's answers to the questions.

> A. Full name: .... ?
>
> B. Birthday: .... ?
>
> C. City, country: .... ?
>
> D. Occupation (in your country/outside class): .... ?
> .... ?
>
> E. Length of time here (in this country/city/school): ....
> .... ?
>
> F. Reason(s) for studying English: ....
> .... ?
>
> G. Plans for the future: ....
> .... ?
>
> H. Free-time activities: ....
> .... ?

Activity B: Writing a letter about your partner

Write a letter to your family or to a good friend. Write about your partner. Use this framework for your letter.

Dear _____ ,

    I (don't/doesn't/aren't) have much time to write now, but I want to (say/said/ saying) hello.   I (am/is/are) starting my English class at (school).   There (is/are) (number) students in my class.   Let me tell you about one of them.

    (full name) is from (city, country).   (first name) was born (on/in/at) (year).   (she/he) is (a/an) (occupation).   (first name) has been here for (number) months.   In the future (she/he) plans to _____.   (first name) and I will spend (number) hours together each week in this class.   Maybe we will become good friends.

    I have to stop now.   I hope you are doing well.   Say hello to _____ for me.   I miss you.

                       (warmly/fondly/love),

                       (sign your name)

(date) at top right of box

Activity C: Writing a letter about yourself

1. Work with your class. Talk about this framework for a letter to your teacher. Compare it with the letter in Activity B. What are the similarities? What are the differences?

2. Write a letter about yourself to your teacher. Use this framework. Add the parts that are necessary in a letter.

    My name is _____.   I am from _____.   (Birthday).   (Occupation).   (Length of time here).   My mailing address is _____.*   My phone number is _____.**   [OR   I don't have a phone.   OR   I will have a phone (when?) .]   (Reasons for studying English).   (Plans for the future).   (Free-time activities).

*Include the zip code or postal code.

**Include the area code.

1.2 THE BANK ROBBERY: *Picture composition*

Activity A: Matching sentences with pictures

Match each sentence with a picture on page 4, and put the number of the picture (1, 2, 3, or 4) beside the sentence. If a sentence describes more than one picture, use the number of the first appropriate picture.

_____ A. The bank director gives the woman a reward.

_____ B. The woman is making a deposit and cashing a check.

_____ C. She stops him.

_____ D. This man walks to a window.

_____ E. A woman and her grandson are in the bank.

_____ F. The lady hits him with her umbrella.

_____ G. He gets seven balloons from the bank director.

_____ H. He takes two bags of money.

_____ I. A man with a hat is walking in.

_____ J. He starts to run away.

_____ K. A crowd watches.

_____ L. He pulls out a gun.

_____ M. Her handbag and her umbrella are on her arm.

_____ N. She looks happy to get the money.

_____ O. The boy has a balloon on a string.

_____ P. A policeman takes the robber away.

_____ Q. His picture is on the bulletin board.

_____ R. Her grandson also has a smile on his face.

_____ S. He shows a note that asks for money.

Activity B: Putting the sentences in order

Use the sentences in Activity A. Decide which sentence about picture 1 is the first sentence in the story. Put "1A" in the blank beside it. Put "1B" beside the second sentence. Continue with the other sentences about picture 1. Then do the same with the sentences about pictures 2, 3, and 4. Check your answers with the class.

Activity C: Writing the story

Use the sentences and answers in Activities A and B. Write the sentences in the correct order to make a paragraph that tells the story. Use the composition format on page 6.

1.3   REVISING: Format

Activity A: Learning vocabulary about format

This paper has a good format. All readers, including teachers, like papers that have a good format. Identify the parts of this paper. Fill in the blanks with the words beneath the paper.

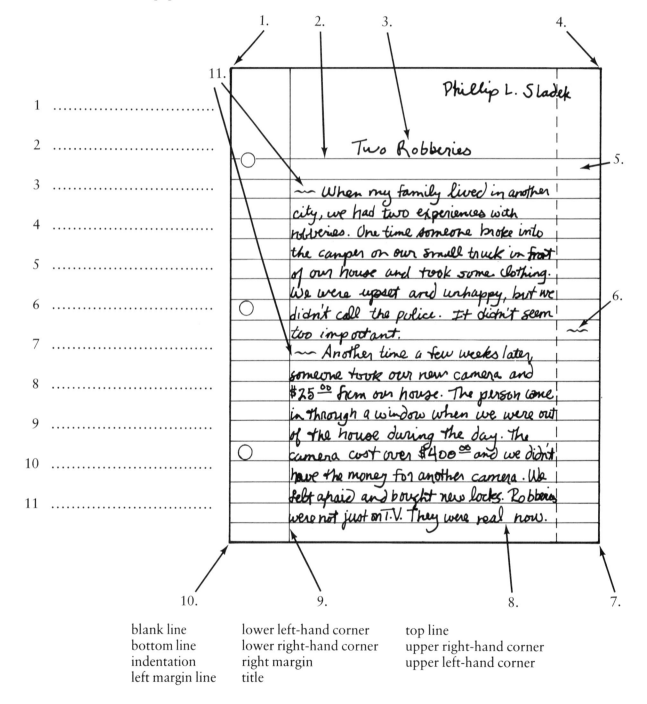

blank line	lower left-hand corner	top line
bottom line	lower right-hand corner	upper right-hand corner
indentation	right margin	upper left-hand corner
left margin line	title	

Activity B: Finding mistakes in format

This writer made nine mistakes in the format of his paper. Can you find them? Write the mistakes in the blanks. Use the vocabulary in Activity A.

When my family lived in another city
We had two experiences with robberies.
One time someone broke into the camper
on our small truck in front of our house
and took some clothing. We were upset and
unhappy but we didn't call the police. It didn't seem
too important. Another time a few weeks later
someone took our new camera and
$25.⁰⁰ from our house.
The person came in through a window when
we were out of the house during the day.
The camera cost over $400.⁰⁰, and we
didn't have the money for another camera.
We felt afraid and bought new
locks.
Robberies were not just on T.V. They were
real now.

Phillip / Sladek

1. ....
2. ....
3. ....
4. ....
5. ....
6. ....
7. ....
8. ....
9. ....

1.4   AN UNSUCCESSFUL CRIME: Practice text

Activity A: Working with pronouns and verbs

The Bank Robbery

[1]A woman and ▲ grandson ★ in the bank. [2]The woman ★ making a deposit and cashing a check. [3] ▲ handbag and ▲ umbrella ★ on ▲ arm. [4]The boy ★ a balloon on a string. [5]A man with a hat ★ walking in. [6] ▲ picture ★ on the bulletin board. [7]This man ★ to a window. [8]He ★ out a gun. [9]He ★ a note that asks for money. [10]He ★ two bags of money. [11]He ★ to run away. [12]The lady ★ him with ▲ umbrella. [13]She ★ him. [14]A policeman ★ the robber away. [15]A crowd ★ . [16]The bank director ★ the woman a reward. [17]She ★ happy to get the money. [18] ▲ grandson also ★ a smile on ▲ face. [19]He ★ seven balloons from the bank director.

▲ = pronoun   ★ = verb

---

1. Some sentences in the story in the box have one or more blanks with a triangle
(▲). Each triangle represents a kind of pronoun called a possessive adjective.
Write the pronouns that are missing in these sentences.

　　1. ....
　　3. ....
　　　 ....
　　　 ....
　　6. ....
　12. ....
　18. ....
　　　 ....

2. Each sentence in the story has a blank with a star (★). Each star represents a missing verb. Write the verb that is missing from each sentence.

1. ....   8. ....   15. ....

2. ....   9. ....   16. ....

3. ....   10. ....   17. ....

4. ....   11. ....   18. ....

5. ....   12. ....   19. ....

6. ....   13. ....

7. ....   14. ....

3. Practice reading the story aloud. Work with a partner. Cover the pronouns and verbs you wrote. Partner A reads the first sentence, and Partner B uncovers the words to check. Then Partner B reads the second sentence, and Partner A uncovers the words to check. Take turns reading, sentence by sentence, until each partner can read all the sentences correctly.

Activity B: Adding details to the story

Rewrite the story in Activity A to make it more interesting. Add these words in appropriate places. You can use some words more than once.

big	long
black and white	new
famous	old
heavy	teller's
little	young

Activity C: Changing the facts of the story

Rewrite the story in Activity A with these facts: A *man* and his grandson are in the bank. The robber is a *woman*.

Activity D: Writing in the past tense

When you tell a story, you usually tell it in the past tense because it has already happened. Rewrite the story in Activity A in the past tense. Your first sentence will be: "A woman and her grandson were in the bank."

1.5 LETTERS ABOUT THE BANK ROBBERY: *Writing from a point of view*

Activity A: Talking about point of view

It is the *day after* the bank robbery on page 4. Everyone is still thinking about the exciting experience.

1. You are the old lady. You are telling your story in a letter to your best friend.
2. You are the bank teller. You are telling your story in a letter to your sister.
3. You are the bank robber. You are telling your story in a letter to your lawyer.
4. You were in the bank yesterday. You saw the robbery. You are writing a statement for the police, telling what you saw.

Discuss with your class how each of these people felt yesterday and feels now. Then discuss how to begin each letter. When you have decided, your teacher will write your first sentences for each letter on the board.

Activity B: Talking about salutations and closings

1. Here are some common salutations for letters. Which one(s) can be used with each of the letters in Activity A?

   Dear Martha,   Dear Officer Reed:
   Dear Sir: Dear Fred,
   Dear Ms. Jones: Dear Mr. Wilson:

2. Here are some common closings for letters. Which one(s) can be used with each letter in Activity A?

   Sincerely,   Warmly,
   Love,   Yours sincerely,
   Very truly yours,   Fondly,

Activity C: Writing the letter

Work with a partner or small group. Look at the pictures on page 4 again. Then close your book. Finish writing one of the letters in Activity A.

1.6 ACTIVE VOCABULARY PRACTICE: *Basic classroom stretch*

There is an Active Vocabulary Practice section in each unit of the book. These sections will help you learn new vocabulary quickly and follow directions easily. The commands in the box show some of the vocabulary you will practice in this unit. In class, with your books closed, you will act out these and other commands as your teacher gives them.

Stand up.
S-T-R-E-T-C-H.
Touch your toes (nose, hair, chin, right eye, etc.).
Touch both knees (both ankles, both shoulders, etc.).
Touch only your left knee.
Touch your right elbow.
Point to your right elbow.
Touch both ears.
Point to both ears.
Point to the blackboard (bulletin board, map, eraser, wastebasket, ceiling, floor).
Point to the upper (lower) left-hand (right-hand) corner of the blackboard.
Point up (down, to the left, to the teacher, to Joe).
Walk forward (backward). Stop!
Smile. Laugh. Frown.
Make a fist. Shake your fist.
Open your hand.
Point to the palm of your hand.
Hit your forehead with the palm of your hand.
Wave good-bye.
Sit down.

1.7 *EXERCISE FOR BUSY PEOPLE:*   *Practice text*

Activity A: Combining sentences

Combine each group of sentences into one longer sentence. Write the new sentences as a paragraph. Omit all numbers and letters when you write.

Exercise for Busy People

1. a. Today John Jones, a typical worker, has a job inside a building or factory.
   b. The building is tall.
   c. The factory is modern.

2. a. He spends eight hours at work.
   b. He rarely uses his muscles.
   c. The hours are busy.

3. a. He exercises only on weekends at a park.
   b. The weekends are sunny.
   c. The park is nearby.

4. a. A worker such as John needs to get exercise.
   b. The exercise is regular.

5. a. Here are two people who know ways to do this.
   b. The ways are easy.

6. a. A lawyer walks to work every day.
   b. She is important.

7. a. She wears a suit.
   b. She wears jogging shoes.
   c. The suit is expensive.
   d. The shoes are old.

8. a. She carries her shoes in her briefcase.
   b. The shoes are nice.

9. a. An employee of a factory takes breaks.
   b. The factory is big.
   c. The breaks are short.
   d. The breaks are in the morning and afternoon.

10. a. He stretches beside a machine.
    b. He touches his toes beside a machine.
    c. The machine is huge.

11. a. Exercise is important to this man and woman.
    b. It makes them feel better.

Activity B: Making changes in the paragraph

Rewrite the paragraph in Activity A to tell about many people. Your first sentence will begin: "Today typical workers such as John Jones have jobs. . . ."

1.8 *REASONS FOR EXERCISING:* *Dictation*

Activity A: Dictation

With your book closed, write the paragraph as your teacher dictates. Then open your book. Compare your paragraph with Form A below.

> Reasons for Exercising (Form A)
>
> Why does a person exercise? Some people exercise for their cardiovascular health. Other people exercise to burn calories and lose weight. They want to look better. Still other people exercise for fun and relaxation. In fact, most people probably exercise for all three reasons.

Activity B: Talking about the dictation

Part I. Practice with the information in Form A.

1. How many sentences tell about reason one? reason two? reason three?
2. What do some people do to relax and have fun?

Part II. Practice with information related to Form A. If your class cannot answer a question, talk about where to find the answer.

3. Everyone has a cardiovascular system. What are the parts of this system? What does "cardio" mean? What does "vascular" mean?
4. Which food has more calories?
   – a potato or a tomato?
   – a salad or a pizza?
   – an apple or a banana?
   – a piece of chicken or a piece of fish?
   – a cup of milk or a bottle of beer?
5. How many calories does the average adult need each day?

Activity C: Adding information to the dictation

Where does this information fit into Form A? Copy Form A and add the information.

1. ...and build firm muscles
2. They enjoy themselves when they exercise.
3. They want to build strong hearts and circulation.

Activity D: Making a cloze exercise

You must study Form A of the dictation to prepare for the dictation quiz of Form B. You do NOT need to memorize Form A. Form B will have the same vocabulary and the same information, but the sentences will be different.

A good way to study is to make your own *cloze exercise*. In the box below, you see an example of a *cloze*. Notice that the student who made this cloze omitted every 6th word. Cover the answers with a piece of paper. Try to fill in the blanks. Check by uncovering one word at a time.

Now make your own cloze exercise using "Reasons for Exercising (Form A)" on page 13. Omit every 5th word. Practice with your exercise.

Reasons for Exercising

Why does a person exercise? ① _____ people exercise for their cardiovascular ② _____. Other people exercise to burn ③ _____ and lose weight. They want ④ _____ look better. Still other people ⑤ _____ for fun and relaxation. In ⑥ _____, most people probably exercise for ⑦ _____ three reasons.

1. Some
2. health
3. calories
4. to
5. exercise
6. fact
7. all

1.9 *EDITING: Subjects and verbs*

Activity A: Talking about sentences, subjects, and verbs

Do you know what a sentence is? You might say it is a group of words beginning with a capital letter and ending with a period. But a sentence is more than that. Every sentence, long or short, has one or more *subjects* and one or more *verbs*. Study the sample paragraph carefully and discuss it with your class. Sample:

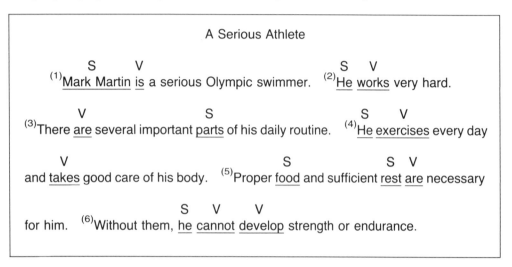

A Serious Athlete

$\overset{\text{S}}{}\;\overset{\text{V}}{}$
(1)Mark Martin is a serious Olympic swimmer.   (2)He works very hard.

(3)There are several important parts of his daily routine.   (4)He exercises every day

and takes good care of his body.   (5)Proper food and sufficient rest are necessary

for him.   (6)Without them, he cannot develop strength or endurance.

Activity B: Identifying subjects and verbs

Underline the subject(s) and verb(s) in each sentence in the next two paragraphs. Then mark each underlined word with "S" for subject or "V" for verb.

Soccer

(1)Soccer is a good form of exercise.   (2)It is becoming more popular in the United States every year.   (3)Boys and girls play this sport for fun and health.   (4)There are no breaks in the game.   (5)Players run constantly and build endurance.

Sports on TV

(1)Baseball and football are popular American sports.   (2)There are many professional teams in each sport, and these teams play games on TV.   (3)These days people are watching less baseball because it doesn't have much action.   (4)But football has lots of action and is an exciting game on TV.

Activity C: Finding subject and verb mistakes

Practice making corrections. Write "S" or "V" in the circles to tell what is missing. Then write the missing words beside the circles.

Football

Football a popular sport. But is dangerous. Players often hurt themselves.

Need special clothing for safety. Helmets and pads necessary.

Activity D: Finding and adding subjects and verbs

1. Bob wrote this paragraph to give his opinion about sports. What is his opinion? Do you agree with it?

2. Bob's paragraph has some mistakes with subjects and verbs. Underline the subjects and verbs, and mark them with "S" or "V." When a subject or a verb is missing, make a circle and write the missing word in the circle. The first two sentences are marked as examples. (HINT: Six sentences are correct.)

The Truth About Sports

V   S
(1)There is too much attention on sports these days.   (2)Most sports useless

S   are

S   V
activities, but some people spend a lot of money on them.   (3)Sports equipment

and tickets for games becoming more expensive every year.   (4)Sports a big

waste of time, too.   (5)Athletes usually aren't very smart because don't read and

study enough.   (6)Are also very bad for the body.   (7)Many people get hurt while

they practicing their favorite sports.   (8)They may pull their muscles or break a

leg.   (9)Finally, sports lovers usually don't have any friends.   (10)Here the

reasons.   (11)Normal people don't like them because they sweat and smell

bad.   (12)They also very boring because are always talking about one thing –

sports.   (13)If they are very good at sports, they often think that they are better

than other people.   (14)Of course, aren't!   (15)In general, the world would be a

better place without sports.

1.10 AN INTRODUCTION TO THE NEWSPAPER

Activity A: Talking about newspapers

Read the questions, and discuss your answers with the class.

1. Do you read a newspaper in your native language? If so, which newspaper do you read? Why? How often?

2. Do you read a newspaper in English? If so, how often? Which paper? Why?

3. Which parts of the paper do you like to read? Which types of articles and columns do you like?

Activity B: Getting acquainted with newspapers

Work with a partner or small group. Look at a recent newspaper in English. Answer these questions about the newspaper.

1. What is the name of the newspaper? What is its date? How much did it cost?

2. How many articles are on the front page? Copy two headlines from the front page.

3. Can you find an article about a robbery or other crime? If so, where?

4. Where is the weather report?

5. Where is the index? What types of things are listed in the index?

6. Is the newspaper divided into sections? If so, what are the names of the sections?

7. Is there an editorial or an editorial section? If so, where is it? How is an editorial different from other newspaper articles?

8. Is there a crossword puzzle? If so, where?

9. Is there an advice column? If so, where?

10. Can you find a cartoon? If so, where? Are there any comic strips? If so, where?

11. Is there a graph or table? If so, where?

12. Where are the classified ads? What are they?

13. Can you find any other advertisements? If so, where? Why does the newspaper have advertisements?

14. Is there a horoscope? If so, where?

15. Are there any advertisements about exercise clothing or classes? If so, where?

Activity C: Making a classroom display about newspapers

Make a display about newspapers for the wall or bulletin board in your classroom. Cut out an example from the newspaper of the items in this list. Tape the items to a big sheet of paper. Label each item with a colored marker. Work with a small group, and put up your display when you finish.

1. name of paper

2. classified ads

3. crossword puzzle

4. political cartoon

5. advice column

6. advertisement for exercise clothing or classes

7. weather report

8. index

9. comic strip

10. graph or table

11. editorial

12. article about a crime

13. headline about . . . .

14. . . . .

15. . . . .

Activity D: Beginning a class newspaper

In this course, you and your classmates will make a class newspaper. You will write the articles and do the artwork. The first step is choosing a name for your class newspaper.

1. Answer these questions with your class or a small group:
   a. What newspapers in English can you buy?
   b. What newspapers in other languages can you buy?
      Can you translate their names into English?

2. Write three ideas for the name of your class newspaper. Share your ideas with the class. With the class, choose a name for your newspaper.

Activity E: Making a masthead for the class newspaper

1. Bring the front pages of some newspapers to class. Look at the top part of the front page. This part is called the masthead. The masthead always gives the name of the newspaper. Look at the names. Are the names in small letters? What information besides the name of the newspaper is in the masthead?

2. Use a pencil, a ruler, and a piece of standard-sized unlined paper. Follow these directions:
   a. Draw a horizontal line ½ inch from the top of the page.
   b. Draw a horizontal line ½ inch from the bottom of the page.
   c. Draw a vertical line ½ inch from the right edge of the page.
   d. Draw a vertical line ¾ inch from the left edge of the page.
   e. Draw another horizontal line 1½ inches below the top horizontal line.

3. In the area between the two horizontal lines at the top of the page, print or write the name that your class chose for its newspaper. Use large, attractive, dark letters. In the same area, use smaller letters to print or write this information: the course, the year, the name of the school, the city, etc.

1.11   *THE STORY OF A CRIME: Composition/newspaper activity*

Activity A: Telling a story about a crime

Have you ever seen a crime? Have you heard about one? What about someone you know? What are the names of some crimes?

Work with a partner. Tell your partner the story of a crime. The crime can be big or small. Tell a personal story if possible. If you don't have a personal story, tell about a famous crime or an imaginary one.

Activity B: Writing a story about a crime (first draft)

Write a story about a crime. Tell all of the story, and give as many details as possible. Work quickly. Follow these rules when you write a first draft:

1. Don't worry about mistakes.
2. Don't erase anything. Cross out words or parts you don't want.
3. Don't ask questions of the teacher or other students. They will be writing, too.
4. Don't worry about vocabulary. Leave a blank or use a word from your language if you can't think of the word in English.

1.12   AN INTRODUCTION TO THE COMPOSING PROCESS

Activity A: Talking about how people compose

Look at the two boxes below. Which box shows what happens when you compose? With your class, discuss what is happening in each box.

Box A

Box B

Activity B: Talking about the steps in the composing process

According to writers, composing is much more than just writing. Composing includes thinking, writing, talking, writing, reading, writing, revising, editing, *and* writing again. On page 21 is one diagram of the composing process. Each big box in the diagram shows a step in the process.

1. Which paper (A, B, or C) is the first draft? the second draft? the final paper? Write these names on the papers.

2. Which frame (1, 2, 3, 4, or 5) shows each step?
   - revising   - writing the first draft
   - collecting information   - editing
   - sharing

   Put these names in the blanks beside the numbers.

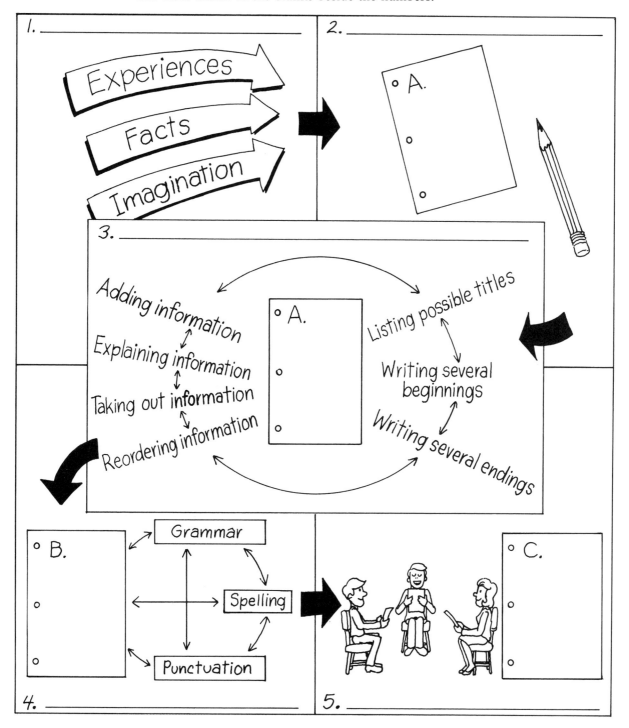

Unit 2 Getting Acquainted

(see Teacher's Manual pp. 14–19)

2.1 MEET MY CLASS: Composition/newspaper activity

Activity A: Learning about averages, minimums, maximums, and ranges

1. Your teacher will read some sentences to you. Listen, and fill in the blanks in the table. Then complete this sentence:

 /

_____ carries his/her books and papers in a _____ .

Situation: Class members use different kinds of bags for their books and papers.

Tom			John	
	Tote bag			Backpack
W18″ × H10″ × D8″	___ × 11″ × 6″	17″ × 12″ × ___		13″ × ___ × 4″
___ lbs.	2 lbs.	2¼ lbs.		___ lbs.
$15	$12			$12

W = width   H = height   D = depth   ″ = inches   lbs. = pounds

2. With a partner make questions and sentences like these:

   – What is the minimum depth? 3½ inches
   – What is the maximum depth? 8 inches
   – The bags range in depth from 3½ inches to 8 inches.

   Talk about *width*, *height*, *weight*, and *price*.

3. Test yourself. Complete these sentences:

   a. The bags range in _____ from 1 to 2¼ pounds.

   b. The bags _____ in width from ____ to 18 inches.

c. The bags range in _____ from 10 inches to 17 inches.

d. The bags _____ in price from _____ to _____.

e. The bags range _____ depth _____ 3½ inches _____ 8 inches.

4. Calculate the following averages with a partner. Follow the example if you need help.

a. average width: _____

b. average height: _____

c. average weight: _____

d. average price: _____

Example: What is the *average* depth?
1. Add the depths:
   8 + 6 + 3.5 + 4 = 21.5
2. How many bags are there? 4
3. Divide 21.5 by 4: 21.5 ÷ 4 = 5.4
   The average depth is 5.4 inches.

Activity B: Working with paragraph organization

1. Match each topic with one of the sentences about an English class.

age   marital status   size of hometown
length of time here   native languages   total number of countries and continents
living situation   occupations   total number of students

.... These students come from cities and towns that range in size from 1,000 to 4 million people.

.... Four of the students are married. Six are single.

.... In their countries they had various occupations. For example, five were students. One was a doctor. Another was a secretary, and another was a mechanic.

.... Ten students, five males and five females, are in the evening English class at West Community College.

.... One student has been here for six years. Another student has been here only two weeks. The average length of time here is four months.

.... They speak the following native languages: Japanese, Spanish, Russian, French, and Swahili.

.... The students range in age from 16 to 55 years. The average age is 32.

.... They come from six countries in Africa, North America, and Europe.

.... Three students live alone. One student lives with a roommate. The other students either live with their spouses and/or with relatives.

⟫→

2. Organize the sentences to make a paragraph.

   a) Which sentence should be first? Why?
   b) Are some of the topics related? That is, do some sentences talk about similar things?
   c) In the left margin write "1" beside the first sentence, "2" beside the second sentence, etc.
   d) Why did you put the sentences in this order? Explain your reasons to the class.

Activity C: Using a chart to collect information

1. Make an information chart on a piece of notebook paper. Follow these instructions.

Instructions for Making Individual Information Charts

A. 1) Fold your paper into thirds (like folding a letter for an envelope).
   2) Fold the paper into thirds AGAIN.
   3) Unfold the paper.
   4) Draw a line along each fold. (How many lines are you going to draw? EIGHT)

B. 1) Fold your paper in half LENGTHWISE.
   2) Fold your paper in half lengthwise AGAIN.
   3) And, AGAIN.
   4) Unfold your paper.
   5) Draw a line along each fold. (How many lines are you going to draw? SEVEN)

C. 1) IMPORTANT! TURN YOUR PAPER SIDEWAYS WITH THE HOLES AT THE TOP. (How many holes are there? How many columns? rows? squares?)
   2) In the square in the upper left-hand corner write the heading "Name." Write "What's your name?" in the square *under* the heading.
   3) In the square to the right of "Name" in the top row, write "Age." In the square *under* "Age" write the question you use to ask a person's age.
   4) Continue across the page writing headings in the top row and questions in the second row. Here are the remaining headings: Length of time here, Living situation, Marital status, Native language, Occupation, Name of hometown and its population, Continent.

D. In the third row answer each question about YOURSELF. For example, under "What's your name?" write YOUR name.

---

2. Work with five or six students to fill in the information charts. The first student asks the second student the questions while the other students listen and write the answers on their charts. Then the second student asks the third student while the others listen and write. Continue in order around your circle.

Activity D: Compiling data

Organize the information from the charts in Activity C. Write the totals and averages for your class (or small group) on the summary sheet.

Summary Sheet

1. Total number of people in the class/group: ....
2. Sex: males: ....   females: ....
3. Age: maximum: ....   minimum: ....   average: ....
4. Occupation: number of students: .... List four other occupations: ....,
    ...., ..., ...
5. Total number of countries: ....
6. List all of the continents: ....
    ....
7. Native languages: number: .... List them: ....
    ....
8. Largest hometown: ....   population: ....
9. Smallest hometown: ....   population: ....
10. Marital status: married: ....   single: ....   divorced: ....
    separated: ....   widowed: ....
11. Living situation: alone ....   with roommate (NOT family): ....
    with family members: ....
12. Length of time here: maximum: ....   minimum: ....
    average: ....

Activity E: Writing a newspaper article about your class

Use the statistics from the class summary sheet in Activity D in a newspaper article. Pay attention to organization. Put related topics together.

2.2 *REVISING:* *"Meet My Class"*

Maria wrote the first draft of a newspaper article called "Meet My Class." She read it several times and decided to revise it. She wrote another draft. Read her drafts, and answer the questions.

1. How are the two drafts alike? ....

   ....

2. How are the two drafts different? ....

   ....

3. Which draft is better? Why? ....

   ....

Box A

> Meet My Class
>
> Twenty people are in my English class. They come from eight different countries on four continents. They have five native languages. They range in age from 19 to 35. Fifteen of the students are single, and five are married. Three of the students live alone, and two live with roommates. The others live with various members of their families. They are an interesting group of people.

Box B

> Meet My Class
>
> Twenty people are in my English class. They range in age from 19 to 35. Fifteen of the students are single, and five are married. They come from eight different countries. Nine of the students live with members of their families. They come from four continents. Three of the students live alone, and two students live with roommates. They are an interesting group of people. They have five native languages.

2.3   *ACTIVE VOCABULARY PRACTICE:*   *Mathematics*

Activity A: Simple arithmetic

1. Study the way we write and say these examples.

ADDITION $3 + 2 = 5$ or $\begin{array}{r} 3 \\ +2 \\ \hline 5 \end{array}$ Three <u>plus</u> two equals five.	SUBTRACTION $8 - 1 = 7$ or $\begin{array}{r} 8 \\ -1 \\ \hline 7 \end{array}$ Eight <u>minus</u> one equals seven.
MULTIPLICATION $4 \cdot 25 = 100$ or $\begin{array}{r} 25 \\ \times\ \ 4 \\ \hline 100 \end{array}$ or $4 \times 25 = 100$ Four <u>times</u> twenty-five equals one hundred.	DIVISION $12 \div 2 = 6$ or $2\overline{)12}$ with 6 above Twelve <u>divided by</u> two equals six. Two <u>into</u> twelve equals six.

2. Work each problem and write it as a sentence. With the class, read each problem aloud, and tell what type it is (addition, subtraction, multiplication, or division).

a) $10 + 7 =$ *Ten plus seven equals seventeen (addition).* ....

b) $4 \cdot 5 =$ ....

c) $3\overline{)36} =$ ....

d) $11 - 2 =$ ....

e) $50 \div 5 =$ ....

f) $18,000 \times 1 =$ ....

Activity B: Decimals and fractions

1. Study the way we write and say these examples.

Decimals

a)   3.2 = three point two   *or*   three and two-tenths
b)   3.25 = three point two five   *or*   three and twenty-five hundredths
c)   0.86 = zero point eight six   *or*   eighty-six hundredths

Fractions

a)   ½ = one-half   *or*   a half
b)   5⅓ = five and one-third   *or*   five and a third
c)   7¾ = seven and three-fourths   *or*   seven and three quarters

---

2. Solve each problem. With the class, read the problems and answers aloud.

   a) $1.5 + 2.25 =$ ....   d) $½ + ¼ =$ ....

   b) $2.5 - 1.3 =$ ....   e) $2 - ⅔ =$ ....

   c) $0.5 \times 0.3 =$ ....   f) $5 \div ½ =$ ....

2.4   THE FAMOUS KENNEDYS: *Dictation*

Activity A: Dictation

Write the paragraph as your teacher dictates. When you are finished, compare what you wrote with Form A in the box.

The Famous Kennedys (Form A)

John and Robert Kennedy were famous brothers. They grew up in a wealthy and powerful New England family. Both entered national politics when they were young. John Kennedy became president of the United States in 1960 at the age of 43. Robert became a candidate for president in 1968. Unfortunately, both of them were assassinated.

Activity B: Talking about the dictation

Part I. Practice with the information in Form A.
1. How are John Kennedy and Robert Kennedy related?
2. In what year was John Kennedy born?
3. How were the lives of John and Robert the same? How were they different?

Part II. Practice with information related to Form A. If your class does not know the answer to one or more of the questions, talk about how you could find out the answers.
4. Do you know which city in the United States is the center of national politics?
5. Do you know where New England is? Which states are in New England?
6. Where, when, and how did John Kennedy die? How about Robert Kennedy?

Activity C: Adding information to the dictation

Copy Form A on a piece of paper, and add this information in logical places.

1. Additional information about John Kennedy:

   – John became a senator from Massachusetts in 1953.
   – John was older than Robert.
   – John died in Dallas, Texas, in 1963.
   – John was the youngest person to be elected president of the U.S.

2. Additional information about Robert Kennedy:

   – Robert became a senator from New York in 1964.
   – Robert died in Los Angeles, California, in 1968.
   – Robert was a candidate for president when he died.

Activity D: Combining information

In the box is a paragraph about Ted Kennedy, the younger brother of John and Robert Kennedy. Combine the information about Ted with the information about John and Robert in Form A. Write one paragraph. Begin your first sentence: "John, Robert, and Ted Kennedy were . . . ."

Ted Kennedy

Ted Kennedy is one of the famous Kennedy brothers. He grew up in New England with his brothers, John and Robert. He also entered national politics when he was young. He became a senator from Massachusetts in 1962.

Activity E: Preparing for the dictation quiz on Form B

Study the structure and spelling in Form A. Make your own cloze exercise using Form A. Omit every 4th word. Cover the answers and practice writing the missing words.

2.5   SIMILAR SIBLINGS: *Practice text*

Activity A: Combining sentences

Combine the following sentences to make a paragraph. Omit the numbers and the letters. Use these patterns:

Tom and Bill
Both Tom and Bill
Both men
Both

Similar Siblings

1. a. Bill is a native Californian.
    b. Tom is a native Californian.

2. a. Tom was born in San Francisco.
    b. Tom was born on October 31, 1958.
    c. Bill was born in San Francisco.
    d. Bill was born on October 31, 1958.

3. a. Tom has curly black hair.
    b. Bill has curly black hair.
    c. Tom has dark brown eyes.
    d. Bill has dark brown eyes.

4. a. Tom is outgoing.
    b. Tom loves to tell jokes to his friends.
    c. Bill is outgoing.
    d. Bill loves to tell jokes to his friends.

5. a. They have good builds.
    b. They are very athletic.

6. a. Bill enjoys all kinds of sports.
    b. Tom enjoys all kinds of sports.

7. a. Bill plays football every weekend.
    b. Tom plays on a soccer team.

8. a. At the university, Bill majored in engineering.
    b. Bill made good grades.
    c. At the university, Tom majored in engineering.
    d. Tom made good grades.

9. a. Bill graduated in 1980 with a B.S. degree.
    b. Tom graduated in 1980 with a B.S. degree.

10. How can two people have so much in common?

11. Of course, they are identical twins.

Activity B: Adding information to the paragraph

Where does the following information fit into "Similar Siblings"? Add these sentences in the logical places.

1. They give lots of parties.
2. Bill was the best student in chemical engineering, and Tom was the best student in electrical engineering.
3. They have five older sisters.
4. They also have dark moustaches and often wear sunglasses.
5. Exercise is an important part of their lives.

2.6   *WRITING ABOUT YOUR FAMILY: Composition*

Activity A: Solving riddles about family relationships

Here are two riddles about family relationships. Can you solve them?

Riddle 1

A man is driving in his car when he sees an automobile accident. He stops to help because he is a doctor. He is very upset when he discovers that the injured person is his son. He takes his son to the hospital as quickly as possible. When the boy is taken into surgery, another doctor enters, looks at the boy, and says, "I can't operate on this boy. He's my son!" How is this possible?

Riddle 2

Two women and their daughters are eating in a restaurant. Only three people are at the table. How is this possible?

Activity B: Preparing questions about families

1. Study the vocabulary in the box. Use your dictionary to look up words that you don't know. If you don't understand something, ask your teacher and classmates.

parents/relatives	immediate/extended family
brother/sister-in-law	people
in-laws	retired
aunt/uncle/cousin	sibling
niece/nephew/cousin	spouse
wife *vs.* housewife	

Q. How many people are there in your immediate family, *including you*?
A. There are five people in my immediate family, *including me*.

⟫→

2. Write questions for these cues. Work with the whole class.

---

1. . . . married/single? . . . . ?

   (. . . children?) . . . . ?

2. How many . . . ?

   people . . . . ?

   brothers and sisters . . . . ?

   children . . . . ?

3. Where . . . live?

   parents . . . . ?

   brother . . . . ?

4. What . . . do?

   mother/father . . . . ?

   husband/wife . . . . ?

   brothers and sisters . . . . ?

5. How often . . . get together? . . . . ?

6. Where . . . get together? . . . . ?

7. . . . most important person . . . family?   Why?

   . . . . ?   Why?

Activity C: Collecting information about families

1. Use the questions you wrote in Activity B to ask about your teacher's family. Try to remember as much as you can, but don't write anything.

2. Bring snapshots (photos) of people in your family to class. Tell a partner about your snapshots and answer questions about them. Find out about your partner's family. Use the questions from Activity B. Try to remember as much as you can, but don't write anything down.

Activity D: Writing to show what you have learned

Test yourself. What did you learn in Activity C? Answer these questions. Check with your teacher and your partner to find out if you remembered correctly.

a. List two things that you learned about your teacher's family.

   1. . . . .

   2. . . . .

b. List three things that you learned about your partner's family.

1. ....

2. ....

3. ....

c. How are your family and your partner's family alike?............................

....

d. How are your family and your partner's family different? ....

....

Activity E: Writing about your family (first draft)

Without your dictionary, write as much as you can about your family in fifteen minutes. Then spend five minutes reading your work and using your dictionary if you need to.

2.7 REVISING: "Meet My Family"

William wrote a composition called "Meet My Family." He wasn't happy with his first draft, so he wrote another one. Read his two drafts, and answer the questions.

1. How are the two drafts alike? ....

....

2. How are the two drafts different? ....

....

3. Which draft is better? Why? ....

....

Box A

> #### Meet My Family
>
> My parents live in a small town. My younger sister lives at home and goes to high school. My older sister lives in the capital with her husband and studies chemistry at the university. My father works hard as an auto mechanic. My mother teaches elementary school. On Saturdays she works as a secretary. For relaxation my father likes to cook and watch TV. My mother is very busy, but she writes me every week. We sometimes get angry, but we love each other very much. Every person in my family is nice and a little crazy.

⟫→

Box B

Meet My Family

My parents live in a small town. My father works hard as an auto mechanic. For relaxation he likes to cook and watch sports on TV. My mother teaches elementary school. On Saturdays she works as a secretary. She is very busy, but she writes me every week. My younger sister lives at home and goes to high school. My older sister lives in the capital with her husband and studies chemistry at the university. Every person in my family is nice and a little crazy. We sometimes get angry, but we love each other very much.

2.8   *EDITING: Editing symbols*

Activity A: Using editing symbols to make corrections

These students wanted help with some sentences, so their teacher marked the sentences with correction symbols. Help the students by making the corrections. Write each sentence again.

WW	= wrong word		/	= Omit this.
WF	= right word but wrong form		⌣	= Add a word.
sp	= spelling error		SV agr	= subject-verb agreement
prep	= preposition (for example: in, on, at, under)		⌐	= Change the order of these words.
#	= number; singular ↔ plural			

                    WW
1. My younger sister has ten years old.

....

                     ⓥ
2. My older sister ^working.

....

        SV agr   WW
3. My father work on the city.

....

4. $\overset{\bigcirc}{\underset{\wedge}{}}$ Are four people in my family.

....

5. My br$\overset{\text{SV agr}}{\text{other stu}}$dy hard.

....

6. They play with h$\overset{\text{WF}}{\text{e}}$.

....

7. I $\overset{\text{SV agr}}{\text{has}}$ many uncles a$\overset{\text{SP}}{\text{n}}$ aunts.

....

8. She $\overset{\text{SV agr}}{\text{live}}$ at t$\not{h}$e home.

....

9. There are $\overset{\text{prep}}{\underset{\wedge}{\text{my family}}}$ twenty pe$\overset{\#}{\text{oples}}$.

....

10. My fathers are g$\overset{\text{WW}}{\text{oods}}$, especially my $\overset{\#}{\text{mother}}$.

....

11. We are l$\overset{\text{WF}}{\text{ive}}$ in Toronto now.

....

12. In my family there are three people: my father, my mother, and m$\overset{\text{WF}}{\text{y}}$.

....

Activity B: Marking mistakes with editing symbols

Each of these sentences has one mistake. Find the mistake, and mark it with the appropriate editing symbol from Activity A.

1. My family have ten people.

2. My oldest brother in the university.

3. My aunt live with my parents.

4. I have two sisters and three brother.

5. My sister studying medicine.

6. My children live now with me.

7. My father has eighty years old.

8. My old sister has three sons.

9. My huband is a student, too.

10. My sisters are work in the city.

2.9 FAMILIES AND FRIENDS AT THE BEACH: Picture composition

Activity A: Matching sentences and pictures

Each sentence tells something about a picture on page 36. In each blank write the number of the correct picture (1, 2, 3, or 4).

_____ A. People are playing volleyball, and someone is water-skiing.

_____ B. The ice chest is in the shade of the beach umbrella.

_____ C. A boy is building a sand castle.

_____ D. A dog is sitting beside a bag of charcoal.

_____ E. A woman in sunglasses is unpacking her car.

_____ F. A woman is taking a nap in her beach chair.

_____ G. People are waving to each other.

_____ H. Two kites are flying in the sky.

_____ I. A man is packing his car.

_____ J. A lifeguard is watching the swimmers.

_____ K. A ship is passing by.

_____ L. Several people are fishing from a boat.

_____ M. A sailboat with a flag is sailing in the distance.

_____ N. People are sunbathing to get a tan.

_____ O. A man with a beard is driving away with a child in the back seat.

_____ P. The garbage cans are full.

_____ Q. A man is cooking hot dogs and hamburgers on a barbecue grill.

_____ R. Someone is upside down in the water.

_____ S. A girl in a dotted swimsuit is holding a pail and a big shell.

_____ T. A beach umbrella is leaning against the side of a car.

Activity B: Planning several stories

The pictures on page 36 give a lot of information, but *you* make them tell a story. In fact, you can make them tell *several* stories. Use the pictures and your *imagination* to fill in the chart. Work with a partner or small group.

	Who?	*Where?*	*When?*	*Why?*
Story One	people who work together		They get together one time every summer.	to meet everyone's family; to get acquainted *outside* work
Story Two	former neighbors			by accident; to get out of the city
Story Three		near Miami	the last day of the summer season	
Story Four				

Activity C: Evaluating possible titles

Here are nine possible titles for Story One. Which titles do you like the most? Why? Which titles do you like the least? Why? Can you think of other possible titles?

The Beach	A Picnic	A Beach Party
A Day at the Beach	A Nice Day	My Favorite Day Last Summer
A Picnic at the Beach	Fun at the Beach	The Worst Company Picnic

Activity D: Developing characters and plot

Look again at the pictures on page 36. Write three possible answers to each question.

a) Who are the <u>man with a beard</u> and the <u>girl with bows in her hair</u>?

1. ....

2. ....

3. ....

b) If they are father and daughter, why isn't Mom there?

1. ....

2. ....

3. ....

Activity E: Creating your own beach story

1. With your class look again at the chart in Activity B. Write a first sentence for each story that you planned.
2. Work alone. Look at the pictures and the first sentences. Choose ONE story and finish writing it, but DO NOT choose the same story as the classmates near you. Use your imagination and have fun!

2.10   A DAY WITH DAD: Practice text

Activity A: Discussing the paragraph

"A Day with Dad" is one person's story about the beach. Read these questions and look for the answers in the story.

1. Who does Becky probably live with? ....

2. Do Becky and Mike spend every weekend together? ....

3. Where did the Holts and the Browns first meet? ....

4. Which word in the story tells you that there are many people at the beach?

    ....

5. Which two words tell you that Becky and Mike did not plan to meet the Holts

    at the beach? .... , ...

A Day with Dad

Becky Brown's parents are divorced. Becky spends every other weekend with her father, Mike. One Saturday, Becky and Mike decide to go to a beach, and there they get a surprise. Their former neighbors, the Holts, are unpacking the next car. What a coincidence! Everyone waves hello and decides to spend the day together. Mr. Holt finds a spot for them on the crowded beach. During the day some people in the crowd sunbathe to get a tan. Other people swim and play in the water. Still others listen to the radio or pick up shells. Becky covers Mike with sand. The Holts' son, Jimmy, builds a sand castle. Mrs. Holt gets a sunburn. When everyone gets hungry, Mike puts on a chef's hat and cooks hot dogs and hamburgers. Kites and birds fly over the picnic. The families eat and eat. Finally, everyone cleans up, packs the cars, and says good-bye. Becky hugs Mike and falls asleep on the way home.

Activity B: Adding details to the paragraph

Make the story more interesting to read. Rewrite the paragraph, and add the following adjectives. You can use some of the words in more than one place.

bad	delicious	nice	warm
big	favorite	short	wonderful
colorful	hot	tall	

Activity C: Making changes in the paragraph

Becky is an adult now. She remembers a favorite trip to the beach when she was a child. Write her story. Here are the first two sentences: "My parents are divorced. When I was a child, I spent every other weekend with my father, Mike. One Saturday, we . . ."

2.11 BEGINNING THE FAMILY HISTORY PROJECT: *Composition*

Activity A: Introduction

Read this introduction to the family history project with your class. Talk about the questions in it with a partner. Then write your answers to the questions at the end.

Introduction to the Family History Project

Some people are very interested in history; some are not. But most people are very interested in the history of their own families and ask questions about their ancestors: "Where did I come from? Who were my grandparents, my great-grandparents, my great-great-grandparents? What did they do? How did they live?"

Do you know a lot or a little about your ancestors? Which relatives were living when you were born? Which are still living? How many *other* generations of your ancestors do you have any information about? Where did you get this information? Is anyone in your family especially interested in the history of your family? What kinds of family records does your family have? Do you wish you had more information about your ancestors? How can you make sure the future members of your family will know about the history of your family?

In this course, you will write a piece of family history <u>for</u> a future member of your family – maybe your son or daughter, your grandson or granddaughter, your niece or nephew, your cousin. You may write for someone who is very young today, or you may write for someone who has not been born yet.

You will write <u>about</u> one family member, preferably someone who is dead now, but that you know about – perhaps a grandparent, a great-grandparent, an aunt or uncle, or a parent. You must choose a family member that your future reader did not know well.

In this course, you will write about your family member several times and in several different ways. For example, you will write about his or her daily routine, an important place in his or her life, his or her personality and physical appearance, important events in his or her life, and other general biographical information.

Near the end of this course, you will use all these pieces to make one special composition about your family member. You, your classmates, and your teacher will read each other's compositions. You will work together to write clear, interesting pieces of family history. It will be an adventure for you – and for your future reader!

1. Who do you want to write <u>FOR</u>? This person will be your future reader: . . . .

. . . . (name and/or relationship to you) . . . .

2. Who do you want to write <u>ABOUT</u>?

   Name: . . . .

   Relationship to you: . . . .

   Date of death: . . . .   Age at death: . . . .

Activity B: Writing your first thoughts

Write about your family member. Write as much as you can. Do not worry about making mistakes. Write about why you chose this family member for the family history project. Then write everything you know and remember about this person.

Activity C: Working with a fact sheet

This is a fact sheet for collecting information about your family member. Compare your "first thoughts" paper from Activity B with the fact sheet. How many blanks on the fact sheet can you fill with information from your paper? Put a checkmark (√) beside these items and fill in the blanks. Then fill in as many other blanks as possible. Talk with your class about where and how you can get the facts you do not know now.

Fact Sheet About Your Family Member

1. Family member's FULL name: ....

2. Date of birth: .... Place of birth: ....

3. Father's FULL name: ....

4. Father's occupation: ....

5. Mother's FULL name: ....

6. Mother's occupation: ....

7. Number of brothers: .... Number of sisters: ....

    Order of birth (oldest? youngest?): ....

8. Number of years of education: ....

9. Spouse's FULL name: ....

10. Date of marriage: .... Place of marriage: ....

11. Number of sons: .... Number of daughters: ....

12. Occupation: ....

13. Date of death: .... Place of death: ....

    Cause of death: ....

14. Brief description (personality & appearance): ....

    ....

    ....

15. Interests: ....

    ....

16. Community service activities: ....

    ....

17. Famous quotations: ....

    ....

18. Important events in life: ....

    ....

Unit 3   Getting into a Routine

(see Teacher's Manual pp. 19–25)

3.1   DR. COOK'S DAILY ROUTINE: *Picture composition*

Activity A: Matching

Listen carefully while your teacher tells about each of the 15 pictures in order. Then listen again while your teacher tells about the pictures in scrambled order. This time, in the blanks below the pictures, write the number of each picture when your teacher tells about it.

Situation: Victoria Cook is a young, single woman. She is a doctor and goes to work very early. She gets up about 5 a.m. Every morning she does the same things before work.

1. a) _____   b) _____   c) _____   d) _____   e) _____
2. a) _____   b) _____   c) _____   d) _____   e) _____
3. a) _____   b) _____   c) _____   d) _____   e) _____

Activity B: Writing new vocabulary

Fill in the blanks in these sentences. Each sentence corresponds to the picture in Activity A with the same number.

1. Victoria .... up .... 5 a.m.

2. She .... out .... bed.

3. She .... to .... bathroom.

4. She .... in ....

5. She .... a ....

6. She .... hair.

7. She .... her ....

8. She .... out .... the ....

9. She .... herself .... a towel.

10. She .... hair.

11. She .... her ....

12. She .... her ....

13. She .... on .... makeup.

14. She .... her ....

15. She .... to .... for ....

Activity C: Talking about Dr. Cook's routine

Work with a partner. Practice making questions and answers about her routine. Use this framework for your questions:

What does Victoria do just | before / after | she .... ?

Examples: Q: What does Victoria do just *before* she gets out of the tub?
A: She rinses her hair.

Q: What does Victoria do just *after* she gets out of the tub?
A: She dries herself with a towel.

Activity D: Writing sentences with "before" and "after"

1. There are *two* subjects and *two* verbs in each sentence. Mark them as shown. Circle the words "before" and "after."

   a. (After) Victoria gets out of bed, she goes to the bathroom.

    b. Victoria gets up after she wakes up.

    c. She puts on her makeup after she brushes her teeth.

    d. Before she dries her hair, she combs it.

    e. Victoria puts on her clothes before she goes to the kitchen.

2. Two of the sentences above have *commas*. How are these two sentences different from the others? Change the sentences so the commas are not necessary. Write the new sentences here.

    ....

    ....

3. Complete these sentences. Use a comma when necessary.

    Examples: Before Victoria gets out of the tub, *she rinses her hair.*........

        ..*Victoria rinses her hair*...before she gets out of the tub.

        After Victoria brushes her teeth , *she puts on her makeup.*...

        Victoria puts on her makeup...after she brushes her teeth.

    a. After Victoria puts on her clothes ....

    b. .... before she combs her hair.

    c. .... after she gets out of the tub.

    d. Before Victoria goes to the kitchen for breakfast ....

    e. After Victoria wakes up ....

    f. .... before she brushes her teeth.

Activity E: Combining sentences

Put all of the information in Activity B about Victoria's routine into the framework in the box below. Copy your paragraph on a clean sheet of paper.

Victoria Cook's Daily Routine
Every morning Victoria .... up .... 5 a.m.   After ....
....
.... shower.   .... rinses it before
....   After ....
towel ....
.... makeup.   Then .... before
....

Activity F: Making changes in the paragraph

Victoria's brother lives across town. His name is Victor Cook. He works as a night nurse. He has the same routine before work as Victoria. Last night Victor followed his usual routine. Write about Victor last night. Use the framework in Activity E.

The title: Victor Cook's Routine Last Night
The first sentence: Last night Victor Cook woke up at 9 p.m.

Note: Victoria puts on makeup, but Victor shaves instead.

3.2   JIM STAMP'S DAY: Practice text

Activity A: Learning about Jim Stamp's Day

Fill in the blanks. Work with a partner or small group.

Introduction:

1 Meet Jim Stamp, a handsome man in his forties. For 20 years Jim was a fire
2 fighter (fireman). Then he retired and went to nursing school. Now, Jim and
3 Victor Cook work together. Jim is new at the hospital so he does not have much
4 seniority. He often has to work at night. He describes his working routine.

Jim Stamp's Day

1   I usually wake .... at 8:30 or 9 p.m.   I .... up slowly, take a ....,

2   ...., and get dressed.   I always put .... jeans, a knit sport shirt, and

3   white leather running ....   Then I go to the .... for

4   something to eat.   While I am ...., I talk with my wife, Barbara.   After my

5   meal, I go into .... living room to watch TV with my 13-year-old ...., Mike, and

6   my 15-year-old daughter, Angela.   Soon, it's time to .... for work.   Barbara ....

7   me in the car.   It .... us about 15 minutes to get there.   As soon as I get to the

8   ...., I change into white pants from my locker.   .... I'm ready for work.

1   My job .... at 11 p.m.   I check all .... my patients and give

2   medications.   .... I do paperwork.   While I .... writing, I talk with Victor and

3   Kay, the other night ....   Every hour on the hour I .... around with a

4   flashlight and .... the patients.   I also stop at my locker .... a quick

5   snack of raisins or crackers.   At 1:30 a.m. I take .... coffee break, and .... it's

6   my turn for a lunch break from 4 to 5 a.m.   .... I go to the cafeteria, but other

7   times I .... a nap.   Afterward, I am very .... with blood pressures,

8 temperatures, medications, and more .... Finally, at 7:30

9 my job .... I change back into my jeans and ....

the hospital.

1   I take .... bus home. .... I get to the bus stop, I buy a newspaper. It ....

2 at least 35 minutes to get home, ... I read the paper on the............. As soon ....

3 I get home, I give Barbara a big kiss and .... put on my running clothes. I run five miles

4 and.............. great. After I take a shower and have ...., I frequently ....

5 things around the house. Occasionally, I go .... with Barbara. After lunch, I

6 start to feel....................... At 2:30 or 3 p.m. I go .... bed. Mike and Angela

7 .... home from school about that time. ...., they often forget that ....

8 trying to sleep and make lots .... noise with their radios and records. Too .... it

9 is 9 p.m., and I .... start a new day.

1   I don't like.............. work at night, but I'm the .... nurse at the

2 hospital. I.............. sleep well during the day, so I generally feel ....

3 Most of all, I .... going bowling with my team in the evening. .... a good

4 bowler, but I .... go bowling when I work at night. I .... that next year

5 I ....work more during the ....

Activity B: Working with the facts

1. Read each of the statements carefully. In the blank, write "true" or "false." If a statement is false, change it to make it true.

Examples: a. *False*........ Jim is ~~20 years old.~~ *in his forties.*

b. *True*........ Jim prefers to work during the day.

1. .... Jim is a fireman now.

2. .... Barbara is a young nurse who talks to Jim at work.

3. .... Jim spends a lot of time with his children.

4. .... Jim reads a paperback on the bus home.

5. .... Jim rarely goes bowling when he works at night.

6. .... Jim checks his patients every two hours.

7. .... Jim's children are teenagers.

8. .... Jim's shift lasts eight and a half hours.

9. .... Jim usually wears jeans at the hospital.

10. .... Jim always eats lunch from 4 to 5 a.m.

2. For each answer, write a question about "Jim Stamp's Day."

Examples: a. *What does Jim buy every morning* ....? a newspaper

b. *How old is Jim's daughter* ....? 15 years old

1. ....? Vic and Kay

2. ....? at 1:30 a.m.

3. ....? take a nap.

4. ....? by bus

5. ....? five miles

6. ....? because he
rarely sleeps well during the day.

7. ....? Barbara

8. ....? 35 minutes

9. ....? at 11 p.m.

10. ....? raisins or
crackers

Activity C: Talking about Jim Stamp's day

Work in small groups. Divide the questions among the groups. Take turns asking and answering the questions. Give SHORT answers. After you practice, you will be "experts" and answer your questions in front of the class *without* looking at the book.

1. How old is Jim Stamp? Between ____ and ____ years old.
2. What is Jim's present job? He's a _____.
3. What did he do before he became a nurse? He was a _____.
4. Why does Jim have to work at night? Because _____.
5. When does Jim wake up? At _____.
6. How does he get up? (one word) _____.
7. What does he wear to work? at work?
8. When does Jim talk to Barbara?
9. When does he watch TV?
10. How does Jim get to work?
11. How long does it take Jim to get to work?
12. What does he do as soon as he gets to the hospital?
13. When does Jim's job start?
14. What does he do while he does paperwork?
15. When does he check the patients?
16. What does he eat for a quick snack?
17. When does he take a coffee break?
18. What does he do during his lunch break?
19. When does he finish work?
20. What does he do before he leaves the hospital?
21. How does Jim get home? By _____.
22. How long does it take Jim to get home?
23. What does he do on the way home?
24. What does he do as soon as he gets home?
25. What does Jim do after his shower and breakfast?
26. When does he go to bed? How long does he sleep?
27. What often happens when Mike and Angela come home?
28. How does Jim generally feel? (one word) _____.
29. When Jim works at night, what does he miss?
30. What does Jim want to do next year?

Activity D: Writing about Jim Stamp's day

Write for 10 minutes. Write everything you can remember about "Jim Stamp's Day." Write as much as you can.

3.3   A ROUTINE DAY: Composition

Activity A: Collecting information

Work with a partner. Take turns interviewing each other about your routine day. First, Partner A *closes* the book. Partner B *opens* the book, asks the questions, and takes notes about Partner A's answers. Next, Partner B *closes* the book. Partner A *opens* the book, asks questions, and takes notes on Partner B's answers.

QUESTIONS ABOUT _____ ROUTINE DAY
(your partner's)

1. When do you wake up? Do you get up immediately?
2. What do you do before you go to school or work?
3. When do you leave your home?
4. How do you get to work or school? What do you do on the way? How long does it take you?
5. When does your work or school start? Are you always on time?
6. What do you do at work or school? When do you take breaks?
7. When does your work or school end? When do you leave?
8. Do you go home right away? If not, what do you do afterward?
9. How do you go home? How long does it take you?
10. When do you get home?
11. What do you do as soon as you get home? Do you always do the same thing?
12. When do you eat? Do you cook? How often do you eat out?
13. What do you do in the evening? Do you always do the same thing?
14. When do you go to bed? Do you go to sleep at once?
15. How long do you sleep?

Activity B: Writing about your partner's routine day

Write a composition with the title: _____ 's Routine Day. Use your notes from Activity A. When you finish, your partner will read your composition and tell you if the *information* is correct and complete.

3.4　*VICTOR COOK'S BREAKFAST:*　*Practice text*

Do you remember Victor Cook? What happens *after* he goes to the kitchen? It is 9:30 p.m. Let's see what Victor is doing now.

Victor Cook's Breakfast

[1]It is 9:30 p.m.　[2]Victor Cook is fixing breakfast before he leaves for work. [3]He is toasting bread in the oven.　[4]He is stirring eggs with one hand.　[5]He is pouring coffee, milk, and juice with the other.　[6]At the same time he is watching the news on TV.　[7]He is also listening to the weather report on the radio.　[8]But he really isn't paying much attention to these things.　[9]He is thinking about his girlfriend, Ellen.　[10]She lives in another city.

Activity A: Writing about Victor's breakfast routine

Victor does the same thing every evening. Write about his daily breakfast routine. Omit the numbers.

The first sentence:　Every night at 9:30 p.m. Victor fixes breakfast before he leaves for work.

Activity B: Writing about Victor's breakfast last night

As usual Victor did the same thing last night. Write about his breakfast then. Omit the numbers.

The first sentences:　Last night Victor fixed breakfast before he left for work. He toasted bread in the oven.

3.5 ACTIVE VOCABULARY PRACTICE: Shapes and symbols

Match the symbols and shapes with their names.

a) _____ ?

b) _____ ○

c) _____ Mr.

d) _____ □

e) _____ %

f) _____ good-bye

g) _____ B

h) _____ b

i) _____ ☆

j) _____ *

k) _____ △

l) _____ $

m) _____ :

n) _____ √

o) _____ 98.6

p) _____ #

q) _____ =

r) _____ ▭

s) _____ ,

t) _____ IV

u) _____ !

v) _____ ( )

w) _____ ♡

x) _____ ◇

1) asterisk

2) a capital letter

3) checkmark

4) circle

5) colon

6) comma

7) decimal point

8) diamond

9) dollar sign

10) equal sign

11) exclamation mark

12) heart

13) hyphen

14) a lower-case letter

15) number sign

16) parentheses

17) percent sign

18) period

19) question mark

20) a roman numeral

21) rectangle

22) square

23) star

24) triangle

3.6 *EDISON'S TYPICAL WORKING DAY:*   *Dictation*

Activity A: Dictation

Write the paragraph as your teacher dictates. When you are finished, compare what you wrote with Form A in the box.

Thomas Alva Edison
1847–1931

Edison's Typical Working Day (Form A)

How did Thomas Edison make over 1,000 inventions? He frequently worked twenty hours out of twenty-four and stopped only for short naps. He ate irregular meals, drank too much coffee, and smoked too many cigars. Despite his unusual daily routine, he lived actively to the age of 84.

Activity B: Talking about the dictation

Part I. Practice with the information in Form A.

1. How much sleep did Edison get in 24 hours? How did he sleep?
2. Did Edison eat regularly? What did Edison like to drink?
3. Why was Edison famous?
4. When was Edison born? When did he die?

Part II. Practice with information related to Form A. If your class does not know the answer to one or more questions, talk about how you could find out the answers.

5. Can you name some of Edison's inventions?
6. Did Edison have a healthy daily routine? Why or why not?
7. The word "despite" shows contrast. Can you write the last sentence in Form A in a different way? Use the word "but."
8. Edison was an inventor. Can you name any other famous inventors?

Activity C: Adding information to the dictation

Where does the following information fit into Form A? Copy Form A on a piece of paper and add these sentences and phrases in the logical places.

1. ... including the electric light bulb and the phonograph.
2. He said, "Genius is one percent inspiration and ninety-nine percent perspiration."
3. He dressed carelessly and shaved only when he had time.

Activity D: Studying for the dictation quiz on Form B

Study the structure and spelling in Form A. Make your own cloze exercise by omitting every 5th word. Cover the answers, and practice writing the missing words. Then uncover the answers and check your work.

3.7 EDITING: *Fragments*

Activity A: Identifying main clauses and subordinate clauses

A *clause* is a group of words with a subject and a verb. There are two kinds of clauses: main clauses and subordinate clauses. A *main clause* can function as a sentence, but a subordinate clause cannot. A *subordinate clause* is only a *fragment* of a sentence that begins with a word like "before," "after," "if," "when," etc.

Read each clause carefully. If it can function as a sentence, write "main clause" beside it, then capitalize the first word and put a period at the end. If the clause cannot function as a sentence, write "subordinate clause" beside it and circle the introductory word or words. (The first two are examples.)

1. (while) he is eating   *subordinate clause*

2. (H)e doesn't like to work at night ⊙   *main clause*

3. the bus is sometimes late

4. when he gets to the bus stop

5. his coffee break lasts 20 minutes

6. after he takes a shower

7. as soon as he gets home

8. it is time to leave for work

9. their radios make a lot of noise

10. before he goes to bed

11. his job ends at 7:30 a.m.

12. if he is late to work

13. after he checks the patients

14. crackers are his favorite snack

15. because he is new at the hospital

Activity B: Writing sentences with subordinate clauses

A subordinate clause is only a *fragment* of a sentence. First, write a subordinate clause that begins with the given word and has a subject and a verb. Then combine your subordinate clause with a main clause to make a sentence. Write true sentences about Jim Stamp's day. (The first one is an example.)

1. AFTER

   subordinate clause: *after he gets to work*

   sentence: *Jim changes his clothes after he gets to work.*

2. BEFORE

   subordinate clause: ....

   sentence: ....

   ....

3. BECAUSE

   subordinate clause: ....

   sentence: ....

   ....

4. AFTER

   subordinate clause: ....

   sentence: ....

   ....

5. WHEN

   subordinate clause: ....

   sentence: ....

   ....

6. WHILE

   subordinate clause: ....

   sentence: ....

   ....

Activity C: Finding fragment mistakes

This is the editing symbol for sentence fragment mistakes: ( )^F. If a subordinate clause begins with a capital and ends with a period, it is a fragment.

Here is the paragraph that one student wrote about her partner's daily routine. There are 6 fragment mistakes in her paragraph. The first one is marked as an example. Find 5 more fragment mistakes and mark them in the same way.

Glenda's Routine

(After Glenda wakes up.)^F She gets up immediately.   Before she puts on her

clothes, she washes her face.   She eats breakfast.   After she leaves home.

Glenda takes the subway to school.   Before she buys a newspaper.   After her

last class ends at 2 p.m., she goes home.   She usually eats something before

she goes to work.   Because she is hungry.   When she finishes work, Glenda

visits her friends.   Before she goes to bed.   She takes a shower.   She reads a

book.   After she goes to sleep.   Glenda usually sleeps six hours before she

wakes up.

Activity D: Correcting fragment mistakes

Rewrite the paragraph about Glenda's routine in Activity C. Correct all 6 fragments. Add the subordinate clause fragment to the main clause before or after it, or change the subordinate clause into a main clause.

3.8   EDITING: *Editing symbols*

Activity A: Finding mistakes

Lila wrote and revised this paragraph about her partner's routine day. Now she is ready to edit. Read her composition carefully. Then work with a partner. Answer the questions that follow the composition. Discuss your answers with the class.

A Routine Day in Life Joe

1   He wakes up at 6 o'clock in very morning.   He immediately gets up

2   at once.   He washes your face and putting your clothes.   Then he eats

3   breakfast.   After breakfast.   He usullys leave home 7:30.

4   He went to school by the subway.   On the train, on your way to school he

5   reading the newspaper.   It takes he fifteen minute get to school, he at

6   school about five hours, his first class begins at nine-fifteen.   and he last class

7   ends at two.   After he goes home.   When he gets home from school eats

8   some thing.   After he go to work.   Then he watch TV listen music and makes

9   homework and some nights he visiting her uncle or friends.   He

10   12 o'clock go to bed.   before he get a shower.   He sometimes

11   in the bed reads book.   Then to sleep.   He usuays sleep 6 hour.

---

1. Who is Lila's composition about?_____
2. How many times do you find this person's name?_____
3. Can you find a word that is misspelled? On which line(s)?_____
4. Can you find a verb that is not correct? On which line(s)?_____
5. Can you find an example of incorrect punctuation? On which line(s)?_____
6. Can you find a mistake with "after" or "before"? On which line(s)?_____
7. Can you find a sentence that is too long? On which line(s)?_____
8. Can you find a pronoun mistake? On which line(s)?_____
9. Can you find a problem with capitalization? On which line(s)?_____
10. Can you find a sentence fragment? On which line(s)?_____
11. Can you find a sentence with incorrect word order? On which line(s)?_____

Activity B: Learning more editing symbols

Study the editing symbols in the box, and review the symbols in Unit 2 on page 34. Use the editing symbols to correct the mistakes in the sentences. Write the corrected sentences on a clean sheet of paper.

C = Capitalize this word.	*pro agr* = Pronoun agreement mistake.	
¢ = Don't capitalize.	*poss* = Use possessive form.	
P = Punctuation mistake. Add or change the punctuation.	VT = Verb tense mistake.	
ᵖ = Omit punctuation.	*rep* = Repetition.	
¶ = Start a new paragraph.	‿ = Connect. Make one word.	
𝓐̸ = Don't start a new paragraph.	( )ᶠ = Fragment. This is only a part of a sentence.	

1. She usuays watches TV at night.

2. Jim works at home, after he eats breakfast.

3. He gets a shower every morning.

4. She goes to School at 8:00 a.m.

5. He puts his clothes before breakfast.

6. She washes your hair every morning.

7. After she does her homework, she watch TV.

8. After work, he goes home and ate a snack.

9. It takes she thirty minutes to walk to school.

10. (After he goes to bed.)ᶠ

11. She washes in the shower her hair.

12. Then listens to music and does her home work.

13. Last night he visiting a friend.

14. He has two class every mornings.

15. Then he goes to the kitchen afterward.

Activity C: Marking mistakes with editing symbols

Each sentence has one mistake. Mark the mistake with the correct editing symbol.

1. He listens the radio every day.

2. He gets out of bed immediately after he wake up.

3. She drinks coffee in every morning.

4. Before he leaves home he eats breakfast.

5. After he listens to the radio.

6. It takes her two hours to do her homeworks.

7. Yesterday he takes the bus to school.

8. He talks to his teacher before goes home.

9. Before bed, she does your homework.

10. He usually walks at class.

Activity D: Correcting mistakes

Look at Lila's composition again. All the mistakes are marked with editing symbols. On a clean sheet of paper, write the final draft of her composition.

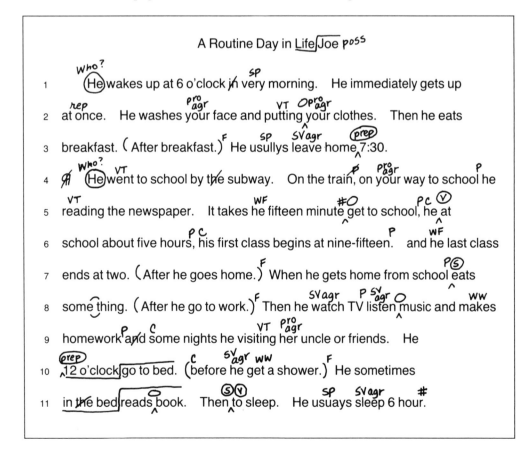

3.9 LETTERS ABOUT A PERFECT ROUTINE: *Composition/ newspaper activity*

Activity A: Talking about perfect routines

Read the following newspaper article carefully. Talk about it with your class. Tell your classmates some things you do not like about your present routine.

PSYCHOLOGY CORNER

Fast way to a new life

DOCTOR NOE ITALL

Are you tired of your daily routine? Are you bored with your typical days? You <u>can</u> change your life. Here is the important first step.

Use your imagination! Imagine that you <u>now</u> have your perfect routine. You wake up at the perfect time and you eat the perfect breakfast. You put on the perfect clothes. Perhaps you have the perfect job and go to work the perfect way. You have <u>exactly</u> the schedule that <u>you</u> like best. Imagine your perfect days <u>in</u> <u>detail</u> and write to me about this routine. Begin your letter like this: "Dear Dr. Itall, I now have the perfect routine for me. Every morning I..."

When you finish your letter, send it to me. I will read it. Maybe I will show it here in my column. So keep reading "Psychology Corner."

Activity B: Imagining a perfect routine

Spend 10 minutes imagining your perfect routine. Write down your ideas. Do NOT write sentences; write only words and phrases. Work quickly. Write as many ideas as you can. Have fun! Be wild and crazy! Use your sense of humor!

Look at your list of ideas about a perfect routine. Put a checkmark (√) beside some of your favorite ideas. Spend five more minutes thinking about the details of your favorite ideas. Write as many details as you can.

Activity C: Writing a letter about your perfect routine

Write a letter about your perfect routine to Dr. Noe Itall. Use the ideas and details in your list. Use humor and imagination. Try to make your reader smile and laugh. Start like this: "Dear Dr. Itall, Now I have a perfect routine. Every morning I...."

3.10 REVISING: "An Imaginary Day"

After Kim wrote the first paragraph of her composition, she read it several times. Then she made some changes and wrote another draft. Read Kim's two drafts, and answer the questions.

1. How are the drafts alike? ....

2. How are the drafts different? ....

3. Which draft is better? Why? ....

Box A

> An Imaginary Day
>
>   At 6:15 a.m. soft classical music wakes me up. For five minutes I stretch and touch my toes. Then I meditate for 45 minutes in a small, quiet garden beside my bedroom. After a hot, lazy shower I put on new jeans and a silk shirt. Next, I have whole-wheat toast, fresh orange juice, and hot tea with my husband and son. After this delicious breakfast I jump into my pink helicopter and fly over the traffic to school. In class I never feel shy when I speak English. After school I push my magic button to cook dinner. I exercise and do my homework. In the evening I am with my family. We go to bed late because we need only four hours of sleep.

Box B

> An Imaginary Day
>
>   At 6:15 a.m. I wake up easily. I stretch and meditate for 50 minutes. After breakfast with my husband and son, I jump into my pink helicopter and fly to school. In ten minutes I am with a wonderful group of classmates. We always do our homework, help each other, and enjoy ourselves, too. In class I never feel shy when I speak English. After school I fly home and push my magic button. It cleans the house and cooks dinner while I swim for an hour. Then I do my homework quickly with my computer. In the evening my family and I talk, read, visit friends, and play games. We have time for everything because we need only four hours of sleep.

3.11 CROSSWORD PUZZLES: Newspaper activity

Activity A: Working a puzzle

Here is a crossword puzzle. Can you work it? Read the questions and write your answers on the grid.

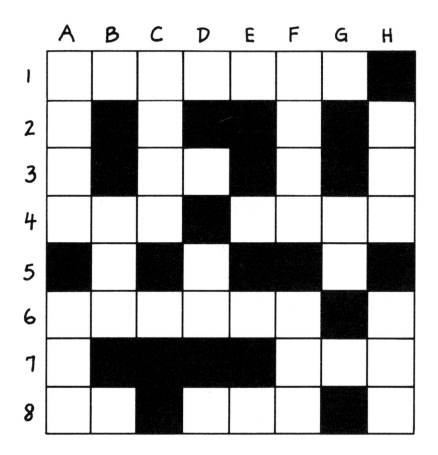

ACROSS

1A   What language are you studying now?
3C   What is the opposite of "off"?
4A   What is a synonym of "unhappy"?
4E   What is another way to write "OK"?
6A   What is after first?
7F   How much is five minus four?
8A   What is the abbreviation of Texas?
8D   What does a chicken lay?

DOWN

A1   What is the opposite of "begins"?
A6   The past tense of "sit" is _____.
B4   What is the plural of "is"?
C1   How do you feel when a friend sends you a long, interesting letter?
D5   What is missing?: I always _____ my homework before I watch TV.
F1   How do you feel when your temperature is 102°F?
F6   What animal likes to chase cats?
G4   What is an abbreviation for morning?
H2   What is the fifth month?
H6   How many fingers do you have?

Activity B: Writing cues

Finish this crossword puzzle. Write one question for each word. You will write 10 questions: 4 across and 6 down. Beside each question, you must write the number and letter (1A, D3, F5, etc.) that tells where to write the first letter of the answer.

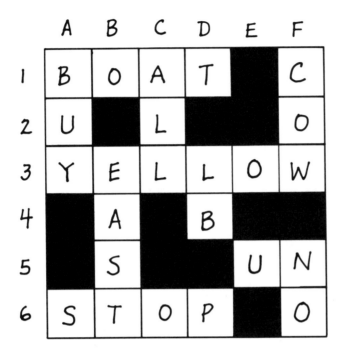

ACROSS

1A   *What do people use to travel on water?*

3A   ....

....

....

....

DOWN

A1   ....

....

....

....

....

....

....

Activity C: Making a crossword puzzle

Follow the directions. Make your own crossword puzzle.

Part I
1. Draw a square on lined paper. Each side needs to be approximately 3 inches long.
2. Draw 9 horizontal lines and 9 vertical lines inside the square. Your grid will have 100 boxes (10 across × 10 down).
3. Write the numbers 1 through 10 to the left of your grid. Write the letters A through J above your grid.

Part II
4. Begin to put words in your grid. After you choose a word, write a question for it.
5. IMPORTANT: Each two words touch in only one place.
6. Blacken all the blank boxes.

Part III
7. On a clean sheet of paper, make a clear, neat copy of your puzzle. Write the question cues, but *don't* put the answers on the grid.
8. Exchange puzzles with a classmate. Have fun!
9. Choose the best puzzle(s) in your class, and put it in the class newspaper.

3.12   FAMILY HISTORY PROJECT – ROUTINE DAY: Composition

Activity A: Thinking about the past

History tells about big events, but it also tells about people's ordinary, usual lives. If you want your future reader to know your family member well, you must tell about what he or she did every day.

Think about your family member's life as a teenager. Complete these sentences, and talk about your answers with the class.

In . . . ., when my . . . . was a teenager, life was
    (year)   (family member)
different because . . .

. . . people didn't have inventions such as . . . .

    . . . .

. . . people enjoyed doing things like . . . .

    . . . .

. . . people worried about . . . .

    . . . .

. . . people valued . . . .

    . . . .

...people didn't have time-savers such as ....

....

...people had more time for ....

....

...women usually ....

....

...men usually ....

....

...young people usually ....

....

...young people rarely ....

....

Activity B: Making notes about routine activities

Imagine *one* typical day in your family member's *teenage* years. Beside each part of the day, list activities that your family member probably did. Use your knowledge *and* your imagination.

in the morning (6 a.m. – 11 a.m.): ....

....

at midday (11 a.m. – 2 p.m.): ....

....

in the afternoon (2 p.m. – 6 p.m.): ....

....

in the evening (6 p.m. – 8 p.m.): ....

....

at night (8 p.m. – midnight): ....

....

after midnight (midnight – 6 a.m.): ....

....

Activity C: Writing about a teenager's routine day

Write about the typical daily routine of your family member when he or she was a *teenager*. (What verb tense will you use?) Use your ideas from Activities A and B as a starting point. Your future reader will know less about the past than you and will be interested in all the details about this daily routine.

Unit 4 Describing Places

(see Teacher's Manual pp. 26–33)

4.1 SOUTH AMERICAN NEIGHBORS: Practice text

Activity A: Working with similarities and differences

1. Find Bolivia and Brazil on the map on page 67. With your class answer the questions: How are the two countries alike? How are they different? List all the similarities and differences that you can see on the map or already know.

2. Talk about Bolivia and Brazil. Use the information in your lists with the following patterns. Which patterns show similarities? Which patterns show differences?

> a) Both countries. . . .
> b) Both Bolivia and Brazil. . . .
> c) . . . , but. . . .
> d) . . . ; however, . . .

Activity B: Combining sentences

Combine the following sentences to make a paragraph. Omit the numbers and letters.

South American Neighbors

1. a. Brazil is a country in South America.
   b. Bolivia is a country in South America.

2. a. Brazil is almost as large as the United States.
   b. Bolivia is only one-tenth as big as the United States.

3. a. Brazil has good farmlands, rich mines, and dense forests.
   b. Bolivia has good farmlands, rich mines, and dense forests.

4. a. Brazil has a long coastline, many rivers, and low mountains.
   b. Bolivia has no coastline, few rivers, and many tall mountains.

5. a. The tallest mountain in Bolivia is more than 21,000 feet high.
   b. The highest mountain in Brazil is under 10,000 feet high.

6. a. Brazil lies south of the equator in the tropics.
   b. Bolivia lies south of the equator in the tropics.

7. a. The climate of Brazil is uniformly warm and humid.
   b. The climate of Bolivia varies with the altitude.

8. a. Indians lived in Brazil for many years before any Europeans arrived.
   b. Indians lived in Bolivia for many years before any Europeans arrived.

9. a. The Portuguese settled in Brazil in the fifteenth century.
   b. The Spanish didn't come to Bolivia until the sixteenth century.

10. a. Today Brazil is an independent nation with many natural resources.
    b. Today Bolivia is an independent nation with many natural resources.

11. a. Brazil is working hard to develop its resources.
    b. Bolivia is working hard to develop its resources.

SOUTH AMERICA

4.2   *THE PROUD STATE OF TEXAS:*   Dictation

Activity A: Dictation

Write the paragraph as your teacher dictates. When you are finished, compare what you wrote with Form A in the box.

The Proud State of Texas (Form A)

Texas is known around the world for its oil wells, cattle ranches, and cowboys. It is also famous for its size. In fact, Texas is so large that it takes about thirteen hours to drive across it. In 1959, however, Alaska became the forty-ninth and largest state. Proud Texans were upset, so they joked that because Alaska was mainly ice, it could melt. According to them, Texas was still the biggest state.

Activity B: Talking about the dictation

Part I. Practice with information in Form A.

1. What is Texas famous for? (Name four things.)
2. How long does it take to drive across Texas?
3. What word means "unhappy"?
4. When were Texans upset? Why?
5. According to Texans, what was Alaska made of?

Part II. Practice with information related to Form A. If your class does not know the answer to one or more of the questions, talk about how you could find out the answers.

6. How many states are there in the United States? (How many stars are there in the U.S. flag?) Which were the original states? Which one became a state just after Alaska? When did Texas become a state?
7. Approximately how many miles (kilometers) is it across Texas?
8. Texas borders four other states and one country. Can you name them *without* looking at a map? Which language in addition to English is spoken by many Texans?
9. What are some famous Texas cities? What are they famous for? Which city is the capital of Texas?
10. Look at the map of Texas. Can you guess in which part of Texas each of these things can be found?

    – oil wells   – rice fields
    – cattle ranches   – pine forests
    – oranges and grapefruit

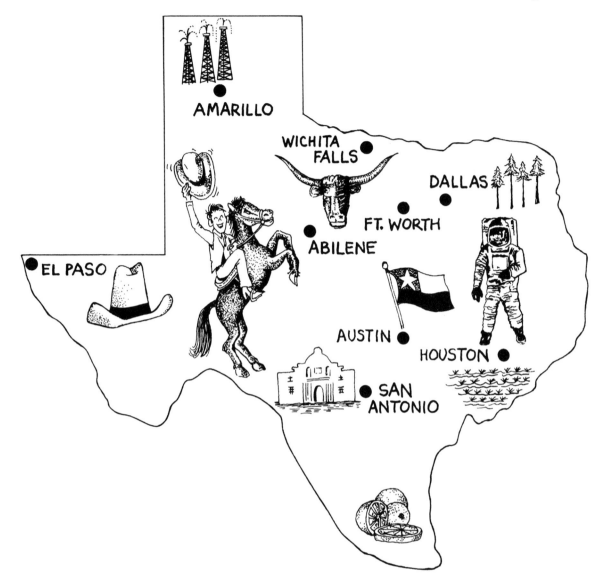

Activity C: Making changes in the dictation

Rewrite the dictation. Substitute each word or phrase in this list for a word or phrase in the dictation with the same or similar meaning.

1. about two days
2. some of them
3. since
4. remained
5. in their opinion
6. everywhere
7. didn't like it at all
8. well known

Activity D: Studying for the dictation quiz on Form B

Study the structure and spelling in Form A. Make your own cloze exercise by omitting every 4th or 5th word. Cover the answers, and practice writing the missing words. Then uncover the answers, and check your work.

4.3   *MY HOMETOWN: Composition/newspaper activity*

Activity A: Finding out about your teacher's hometown

Interview your teacher about his or her hometown. Ask the *underlined* questions in the box. Listen carefully to the answers.

Some Questions About Your Hometown

1. What is the name of your hometown?
2. In what part of your country is it?
3. Describe the geography of your hometown. Is it flat / hilly / in the mountains / in a valley / in a desert / on the coast? Is the land rocky / sandy / good for farming / good for ranching? Are there trees? Is there a river or a lake nearby? Is there a good harbor for ships?
4. Describe the weather and climate. How many seasons are there? What is the weather and temperature in each season? Does it rain or snow? How much? What is the best time of year?
5. How many people live in your hometown?
6. What are the common occupations? What do most people do for a living? What are the principal industries and products?
7. What do people do for entertainment?
8. Is your hometown a good place to visit? Why or why not? What should a tourist see there? What is your hometown famous for?
9. What do you like about your hometown? What do you dislike about it? Does it have any problems? If so, what are they?
10. On the whole, is it a good place to live?

Activity B: Interviewing a classmate

1. Interview a partner about his or her hometown. Use the questions in the box. (*Partner A closes* the book. *Partner B looks* at the book and asks the questions. Partner A answers.) Then exchange roles with your partner.

2. In five minutes, write as much as you can about your partner's hometown.

3. Exchange papers with your partner. Check the information about your hometown. Tell your partner about any mistakes in content that you find.

Activity C: Writing about your hometown

Write a paragraph about your hometown. Use the questions in the box as a guide.

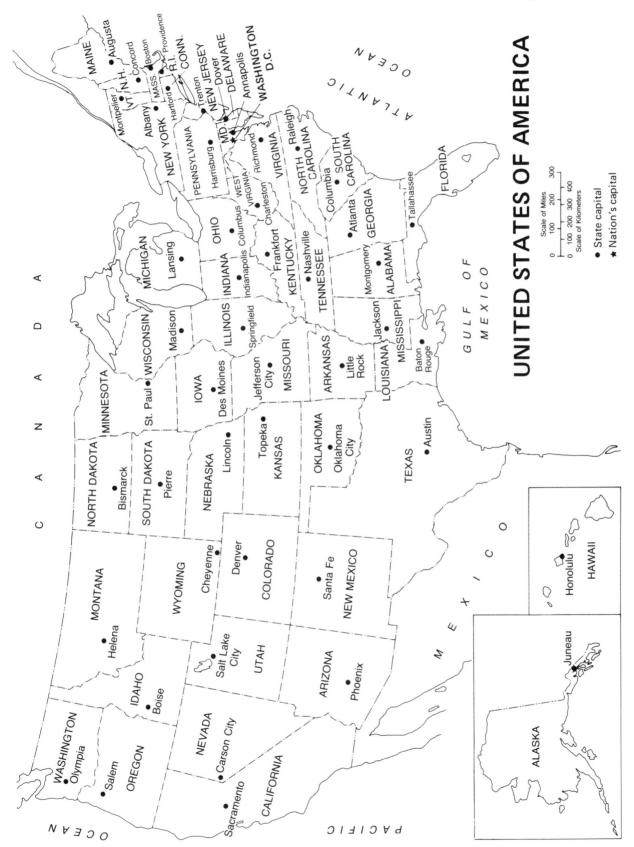

UNITED STATES OF AMERICA

4.4 *REVISING:* "My City"

Stanley wrote the first draft of a composition called "My City." He read it several times. He wasn't sure about it, so he wrote another draft. Read his drafts, and answer the questions.

1. How are the drafts alike? ....

   ....

2. How are the drafts different? ....

   ....

3. Which draft is better? Why? ....

   ....

Box A

> My City
>
> My city's name is Athens. It has good geography and good weather. For example, the climate is nice. It is a big city. Many people live in Athens. They work there in many things, such as different occupations and different industries. The people enjoy different entertainment. They like to do different things for fun and relaxation. I like my city because it has many famous things to see. It also has many museums and good places to visit. In general, all tourists like my city very much. For instance, they like the well-known places to visit. I love my city because it is a good place to live, work, and play.

Box B

> My City
>
> My city's name is Athens. In my city there are four seasons. The best time of year is spring. In Athens live three million people. Most of them work in offices, factories, and stores. My city is a good place to visit because the weather is very good, the people are very friendly, and there are many exciting places for tourists. Athens has many museums. It also has famous things to see. Two examples are the Acropolis and the Parthenon. My city is also well known because many famous people, such as Socrates, Aristotle, and Pericles, lived there.

4.5 EDITING: *Punctuation*

Activity A: Changing meaning with punctuation

Punctuation is important. It can change meaning. Work with your class. Add commas, periods, and/or capitals to each sentence.

1. The travel agent called Joan Gordon Ellen Carter and me.

    a) How many people did the travel agent call? ....

    b) Rewrite the sentence to show that the agent called five people. ....

    ....

    ....

    c) Rewrite the sentence to show that the agent called three people. ....

    ....

    ....

2. Roger was born in France on September 7, 1970 he went to Canada to work with his brother.

    a) What happened on September 7, 1970? ....

    b) Rewrite the sentence to show when Roger was born. ....

    ....

    ....

    c) Rewrite the sentence to show when Roger went to Canada. ....

    ....

    ....

Activity B: Solving a punctuation riddle

Joe had a ticket for a trip from Chicago to Toronto. Add punctuation to each paragraph about Joe to make it true.

Chicago   Toronto

From Place to Place (I)

Joe walked into the plane before the flight attendant closed the door he walked out when the plane landed where was Joe he was in Toronto

From Place to Place (II)

Joe walked into the plane before the flight attendant closed the door he walked out when the plane landed where was Joe he was still in Chicago

4.6 *EDITING: Run-ons*

Activity A: Learning about a "run-on"

Here is a new editing symbol: ( )^R . It means the writer did not use capitals and periods to mark the beginning and end of all the sentences. Rewrite the run-ons as shown in the example:

Example: (The geography in my hometown is interesting, the land to the east is flat and good for farming, to the west it is hilly and rocky.)^R

The geography in my hometown is interesting. The land to the east is flat and good for farming. To the west it is hilly and rocky.

1. (The common occupations in my hometown are university employee and government worker, many people also make electronic equipment, others sell insurance or work in stores.)^R

....
....
....
....
....

2. (For entertainment people like to spend time outdoors, swimming, boating, and fishing are popular, many people ride bicycles for fun, people also have picnics at the lakes.)^R

....
....
....
....
....

Activity B: Finding and correcting problems

1. Cover the symbols. Read each line of the paragraph in the box carefully. Look for the problems. Put a check (√) near each problem.

   Examples:

poss	My city name is Ottawa.
cover→ **s-v agr**	The people has many occupation.

2. Uncover the symbols. Compare them with your checks. Did you find all the problems on each line?
3. Rewrite the paragraph. Make the necessary changes. Use the symbols and checks for help.

COVER↓

WF	My city is a excellent place to
sp, ⑤∧	live. I thing is wonderful. It has
ww, ⑤∧, ⓐⁿᵗ∧	very people. Is important city
⑤∧, sp	because is the center of goberment.
⑤∧, ww	Is also great because of yours
⌐, ᴿ(	museums very famous. The weather
	in my city is nice, in the
⑤∧	summer is warm and sometimes
)ᴿ	rains, in the winter it is cool.
⌐, ⓐᵈᵛ·∧	I very like my city.

4.7   *HOMETOWN WEATHER REPORT: Newspaper activity*

Activity A: Talking about temperature scales

Work with a small group, and then with the whole class. Answer these questions.

$$104°F = 40°C$$

1. Look at the temperatures in the box. What do the small circles mean? What does "F" mean? What does "C" mean?
2. At what temperature Celsius (centigrade) does water freeze? At what point does it boil?
3. What is the boiling point of water on the Fahrenheit scale? What is the freezing point of water on this scale?
4. On the Celsius scale, how many degrees are there between freezing and boiling? On the Fahrenheit scale?
5. Complete the proportion (ratio) between the Celsius and the Fahrenheit scales:

$$\frac{C}{F} = \frac{100 \text{ degrees between freezing and boiling}}{180 \text{ degrees between freezing and boiling}} = \frac{100}{180} = \frac{10}{18} = \frac{?}{9}$$

Activity B: Practicing temperature conversions

When you change Celsius to Fahrenheit or vice versa, you must remember that the Fahrenheit scale starts at 32°, not 0°. Therefore, you must add or subtract 32°, depending on which change you are making. Study the information in the boxes. Then practice making conversions.

To Change Fahrenheit to Celsius

$$\frac{5(F - 32)}{9} = C \qquad \text{OR} \qquad$$ Subtract 32 from degrees of Fahrenheit and multiply by 5. Then divide by 9.

To Change Celsius to Fahrenheit

$$\frac{9C}{5} + 32 = F \qquad \text{OR} \qquad$$ Multiply Celsius degrees by 9, divide by 5, and add 32.

1. Change 100°C to Fahrenheit.
2. Change 32°F to Celsius.
3. Normal body temperature is 98.6°F. What is it in Celsius?
4. Imagine that the weather forecaster on the radio predicted a low tonight of 10°C. What is the predicted low in Fahrenheit?

Activity C: Collecting information

Complete the statements in the box.

In my opinion, the best weather in _____,
                                                          (my city)
_____, occurs in _____ .
        (my country)   (month)

In this month:

a) The skies are clear / partly sunny / partly cloudy / overcast.

b) The daytime high temperature is _____°C (_____°F).

c) The low temperature at night is _____°C (_____°F).

d) The humidity is _____%.

Activity D: Making a weather report

Follow these steps to make a weather report for your newspaper.

1. Draw a square or rectangle in the space available in your newspaper for the weather report.

2. Label it "Today's Weather." (If you have more space available on another page of your newspaper, use the title "Tomorrow's Weather" for a second weather report.)

3. Print in the information about skies, daytime high, low tonight, and humidity.

4. Draw something attractive, such as a sun, clouds, an umbrella, etc.

5. At the bottom print "P.S. If you like today's (tomorrow's) weather, go to _____(city)_____ , _____(country)_____ , in ____(month)____ ."

6. Just below the square, print "Reporter: _____(your name)_____ ."

4.8 *SURVEY OF FAVORITE CITIES: Newspaper activity*

Activity A: Organizing the survey

You and your classmates are going to interview fluent English speakers (native speakers, if possible) about their favorite cities or towns. You will read all of the answers in the class newspaper.

Work with your class. Answer these questions:

1. Which English speaker will each person interview?
2. Where and when will you talk to this person? Will you use the telephone? Will you need to make an appointment?
3. Help the teacher make a list of *who* everyone will interview, *where*, and *when*.

Activity B: Practicing for your interview

With your classmates and teacher, plan and perform possible conversations with the English speaker. If possible, also record and transcribe one or more of these conversations. Include these points in the role plays:

— Practice introducing yourself.
— Practice telling your purpose.
— Practice making an appointment for later if necessary.
— Practice getting the information: What is your favorite city or town? Why?
— Practice what to say when you don't understand or need help.
— Practice thanking the person.
— Practice ending the conversation.

Activity C: Doing the interview and writing it up

1. Interview the English speaker. Write down his or her full name. Check the spelling! Write down his or her answers as exactly as possible.
2. Write a short report on your interview. Include the full name of the English speaker, the time and the place of the interview, and, of course, the English speaker's answers.

4.9   *A TRIP TO TOKYO: Practice text*

Activity A: Making changes in paragraphs

Tina and her husband Ted are now in Tokyo. Rewrite the paragraph to tell about both of them. Begin your first sentence: "Tina and Ted . . ."

A Trip to Tokyo

Tina is spending her vacation in Tokyo. She is wearing her sunglasses and carrying her camera. She is doing everything that tourists like to do. She is visiting museums, shopping in expensive stores, and walking through beautiful gardens. She is also going to famous restaurants. She is staying in the apartment of a friend who is taking her vacation out of the city. Tina is enjoying herself very much, but she is also spending all her money!

Activity B: Writing about her annual vacation

Tina goes to Tokyo every year. Write about her annual vacation. Start with: "Every year Tina . . . "

Activity C: Writing about their annual vacation

Ted goes on vacation with Tina every year. Write about their annual vacation. Begin with: "Every year Ted and Tina . . . "

4.10 ACTIVE VOCABULARY PRACTICE: *Following directions**

Follow the directions in the box. Work by yourself.

Part One

First, take a sheet of paper out of your notebook. Print your name with capital letters in the upper right-hand corner, last name first. Then write the date in the upper left-hand corner, and put the title, "The Seasons of the Year," in the middle of the top line. Finally, number from one to four along the left-hand margin.

Part Two

First, write the names of the seasons of the year beside the numbers. Put "winter" beside number 1, "spring" beside number 2, etc. After that, circle "summer." Underline "fall." Draw a line through "winter." Put an X on number 3. Then draw a rectangle around "spring" and draw a triangle beside "fall." Also, draw a square to the right of "winter," and put a checkmark in the square. Finally, put a check to the left of number 4.

Part Three

First, sign your name in the lower right-hand corner on the bottom line. Next, fold your paper into sixths. Finally, sign your name again on the outside, and write the date above it.

Part Four

Give your paper to the teacher.

**Referred to as Exercise 5 in the Teachers' Notes.*

4.11   CLASS TRIP: *Composition/newspaper activity*

Activity A: Choosing a place of interest

Take a trip with your teacher(s) and classmates. Go to a museum, zoo, park, amusement park, sports event, skating rink, restaurant, interesting neighborhood, monument, tourist attraction, etc. Have a meal together if possible. Speak English during the trip!

1. Work with a partner or small group. Brainstorm about places of interest that would be good for a class trip. Make a list of your ideas:

a. ....   f. ....

b. ....   g. ....

c. ....   h. ....

d. ....   i. ....

e. ....   j. ....

2. Work with your whole class. Share your best ideas from the list. Choose the place for your class trip.

Activity B: Planning the trip

Discuss these points with your class.

– date of the trip
– time of departure and return
– cost (of transportation? of admission ticket? of meal or snack?)
– clothing
– place to eat
– type of transportation
– place to meet
– things to take (camera? umbrella? sports equipment? food? swimsuit?)
– people to invite (other teachers? family members? roommates?)

Activity C: Writing about the trip

After your trip, write a short report that tells where you went and what you did.

4.12   FAMILY HISTORY PROJECT – IMPORTANT PLACE: Composition

Activity A: Making a list of places

1. Read the family history papers you wrote in Units 2 and 3. Make a list of all the places you mentioned.

2. Add to your list other important places in the life of your family member. Think about where this person was born, grew up, went to school, married, raised a family, worked, spent older years, and died.

Activity B: Writing about an important place

1. Choose one place from your list that was very important in the life of your family member. Fill in the blanks.

   a) name of place: ....

   b) # of years spent there: ....

   c) dates there: ....

   d) age while there: ....

2. Write a description of this important place in your family member's life. Be sure to include the information in the blanks.

Unit 5   Describing People

(see Teacher's Manual pp. 34–41)

5.1   *LETTER TO A HOST FAMILY:*   Composition

Activity A: Talking about the advertisement

Read the magazine advertisement. Discuss these questions with your class, and list your ideas on the board:

— What would a host family want to know about a future guest?
— What questions might they ask?

---

*Spend a month
with an American
family*

- new friends
- home-cooked american food
- family life
- conversations in English

It's easy to participate:
Just send a short letter describing yourself. We'll give it to the family chosen for you.

Mail to: American Host Families
              Los Angeles, California

Activity B: Writing a letter about yourself

Answer the ad. Write a letter describing yourself for a host family.

5.2 DESCRIBING OTHER PEOPLE: *Dialog*

Activity A: Learning a dialog

After you learn the dialog orally with your teacher and class, fill in the blanks with the words you learned. Then cover the words and use the picture cues to practice the dialog with a partner.

Situation: Mark and Annie, two friends, are chatting at the laundromat while they are doing their laundry.

1. Annie: Have you ever _____ my sister, Sue?

   Mark: No, but I'd _____ to. _____ she _____ _____ you?

   Annie: Not at _____. She doesn't _____ _____ anyone in our family.

2. Mark: Well, _____ does she _____ _____ ?

   Annie: Let's _____. She _____ long _____ blond hair, _____ brown eyes, and a good _____ .

3. Mark: Wow! She sounds _____ ! _____ she _____?

   Annie: She's smart _____ friendly and _____ a great _____ of _____ .

4. Mark: What a fantastic _____ ! What _____ your sister _____?

   Annie: Hmm ... Lots of things ... country _____ , old _____ , and _____ , but she sprained _____ _____ last week.

5. Mark: Gee, _____ too bad. How _____ _____ now?

   Annie: Oh, she's _____ better. _____ you _____ to meet her?

6. Mark: Yeah. Do you think _____ go out with me?

   Annie: I _____ it! She's happily _____ and _____ three _____ .

Activity B: Studying vocabulary

Answer these questions about the dialog.

1. Which word means "intelligent"? ....
2. Which word means "outgoing"? ....
3. Which phrase means "funny"? ....
4. Which word means "children"? ....
5. Which word is the antonym of "straight"? ....
6. Which is the full form of these contractions?

    I'd ....

    What's ....

    She'd ....

    She's ....

    That's ....

Activity C: Matching questions with their meaning

Find five questions about Sue in the dialog. Copy them beside the appropriate labels.

Interests ....

Personality ....

Physical appearance ....

Temporary condition ....

Resemblance ....

Activity D: Matching questions and answers

Annie asks some questions about Mark's brother. Put the letter of Mark's answer in the blank beside Annie's question.

...... Who does he look like?

...... What does he look like?

...... What is he like?

...... What does he like?

...... What does he dislike?

...... How is he these days?

a) He looks exhausted. He's very busy at work and needs a vacation.

b) Baseball, Italian food, video games, and classical music.

c) He has dark hair and eyes. He's not tall, but he is muscular and has broad shoulders. He's really good-looking!

d) He's a little shy, but he's fun to be with. He's very understanding and has lots of common sense.

e) We don't look much alike. In general, he resembles my father's side of the family, but he has my mother's eyes.

f) He hates being early, and he gets bored with watching TV.

5.3   SURVEY ABOUT THE TYPICAL STUDENT: Newspaper article and thank-you letter

Activity A: Practicing adverbs of frequency

Match the arrows with the corresponding adverbs of frequency. For example: I <u>never</u> eat breakfast. = I eat breakfast <u>0% of the time</u>.

almost always	never	seldom
almost never	occasionally	sometimes
always	often	usually
frequently	rarely	

0%	10%	20%	30%	40%	50%	60%	70%	80%	90%	100%
↑	↑	↑		↑		↑		↑		↑ ↑
①	②	③		④		⑤		⑥		⑦ ⑧

1 *never* ....

2 ....

3 a) ....

   b) ....

4 a) ....

   b) ....

5 a) ....

   b) ....

6 ....

7 ....

8 ....

Activity B: Collecting data

1. Look at the "Typical Student Survey Form" on pages 86–7. You will use this form to interview another student and collect data for a newspaper article. For each of the 25 cues, write a complete question. Work with a partner.

⟫→

2. Answer the questions on the survey form with information about *yourself*. Write your answers in the column "You." Be sure to record answers of "zero," too!

3. Interview another student. Write the student's answers in the column "Your Partner."

4. Work with your class. Compile statistics from *all* of the answers on *all* of the survey forms.
   - For questions such as "weight" and "# of brothers and sisters," calculate the *average* of the answers.
   - For questions such as "hair color" and "transportation," find the total for each possible answer and use the *largest*.

TYPICAL STUDENT SURVEY FORM

	You	Your Partner
1. Name: _____ 　　(first)　　　　　　(last) 1. Name: _____ 　　(first)　　　　　　(last)		
2. eye color (B = blue, Bk = black, Bn = brown, Gr = green, G = gray)		
3. hair color (Bk, Bn, G, R, Bd)		
4. hair type (S = straight, C = curly, W = wavy)		
5. weight (in pounds)　(You don't have to tell the truth!)		
6. height (in feet and inches)		
7. personality (Q = quiet, O = outgoing or talkative)		
8. favorite kind of music (R&R, P, C, T, C&W, J)*		
9. # of brothers and sisters		
10. neighborhood/area of town		

11. type of transportation to class (C, B, Bi, T, W)**		
12. length of time to get to class (in minutes)		
13. # of letters per month to family members in other places		
14. # of phone calls per month to family members in other places		
15. # of movies per month (in a theater)		
16. # of cups of coffee/sodas daily		
17. # of cigarettes/hamburgers/pieces of gum daily		
18. # of hours of TV daily		

*R&R = rock'n roll, P = popular, C = classical, T = traditional, C&W = country and western, J = jazz
**C = car, B = bus, Bi = bike, T = train, W = walk

Answer questions 19–25 by pointing to a place on the line. Then write the percentage in the column at the right.

0%   10%   20%   30%   40%   50%   60%   70%   80%   90%   100%

19. How often .... get up before 6 a.m.?		
20. .... arrive on time for class?		
21. .... eat out?		
22. .... eat alone?		
23. .... to bed before midnight?		
24. .... the radio while you go to sleep?		
25. .... ONLY English all day?		

Activity C: Writing the article

Put the statistics that you and your classmates collected into this framework. Work with a partner. Read the article aloud, and fill in the blanks orally as you read. Write the completed article on your own paper.

> ★ = verb   # = a number   ▲ = adverb of frequency

What is the typical (level? program?) student like? We did a survey of __#__ students to find out. Here is a description of the typical student according to our survey.

The average (level? program?) student __★__ (eyes) and (hair). S/he __★__ (height) and __★__ (weight). S/he __★__ a _____ personality and __★__ _____ music. S/he __★__ from a family with __#__ children and __★__ (in/near) (neighborhood/area of town). S/he __★__ (transportation) to (name of school). The trip __★__ him/her (length of time). Every month s/he __★__ __#__ letters and __★__ __#__ phone calls to family members in other places, and __★__ to __#__ movies. Daily, s/he __★__ __#__ cups of coffee, __★__ __#__ cigarettes, and __★__ __#__ hours of TV. S/he __▲__ __★__ before 6 a.m. and/but __▲__ __★__ on time to class. S/he __▲__ eats out and/but __▲__ eats alone. S/he __▲__ __★__ to bed before/after midnight and/but __▲__ __★__ to the radio while s/he __★__ to sleep. Finally, s/he has some happy/sad/surprising news for his/her English teacher. S/he __▲__ __★__ only English all day.

Activity D: Making changes in paragraphs

Last year the statistics about the typical student were somewhat different. Write another paragraph, and use last year's statistics in the box. Your first sentence: "Last year, the average .... student had gray eyes and straight, red hair."

Last Year's Statistics: The Typical Student

eyes: gray	letters: 3.6
hair: red	calls: 5.3
straight	neighborhood: near the university
weight: 119.6 lbs.	personality: outgoing
height: 5′4¼″	transportation: walk
brothers and sisters: 3.9	length of time to class: 17 minutes

coffee: 1.6 cups
cigarettes: 6.5
TV: 2.3 hours
movies: 1.3
before 6 a.m.: 10% of the time
on time: 95% of the time

restaurant: 80% of the time
alone: 65% of the time
before midnight: 96% of the time
radio: 0% of the time
only English: 45% of the time
music: classical

Activity E: Writing a thank-you letter

Use this framework to write a thank-you letter to the person that you interviewed in the typical student survey. Talk with your class about words to put into the framework. Write your letter on unlined paper. Fold the letter and address it like an envelope. Deliver the letter to your survey partner.

(date)

Dear _____ ,
        My classmates and I really
appreciate _____. We used the
information to _____. We are
sending you _____ and hope you
enjoy _____. Thank _____ for
_____.

                Sincerely,

                (your signature)

your full name
class
room
school

[stamp]

your partner's first + last name
class
room
school

5.4 THOMAS ALVA EDISON: Dictation

Activity A: Dictation

Write the paragraph as your teacher dictates. Then open your book and compare what you wrote with Form A.

Thomas Alva Edison (Form A)

Thomas Alva Edison went to school for only three months, but he loved books, had an excellent memory, and was intensely curious about everything. Almost deaf, this attractive man with pale blue eyes had remarkable energy and determination. He was a practical organizer who constantly asked questions from his childhood until his death.

Activity B: Identifying subjects and verbs

Underline the subject(s) and verb(s) in each sentence in Form A. Mark each underlined word with "S" for subject or "V" for verb.

Activity C: Practicing with the information in Form A

1. How long did Edison go to school?
2. What did Edison like?
3. Could Edison hear well?
4. What did Edison look like?
5. What was Edison like?

Activity D: Adding information to the dictation

Where does the following information fit into Form A? Copy Form A, and add these pieces of information in logical places.

1. in 1931
2. from a childhood accident
3. creativity
4. and a square jaw
5. , especially science

Activity E: Practicing with adjective and noun forms

Here are some words that describe Edison's personality. Decide which word in each pair is a noun (N) and which is an adjective (ADJ). Follow the sentence patterns in the example, and write a sentence about Edison with each word.

1. a. (creative)   ADJ *Edison was creative.*
    b. (creativity)   N *Edison had remarkable creativity.*
2. a. (curiosity)   ....
    b. (curious)   ....
3. a. (determined)   ....
    b. (determination)   ....
4. a. (energetic)   ....
    b. (energy)   ....
5. a. (self-confidence)   ....
    b. (self-confident)   ....

Activity F: Matching

Here is some more interesting information about Edison. Match the words in the list with the sentences in the box.

a) energetic
b) creative
c) a good organizer
d) great determination

e) little formal education
f) remarkable
g) intense curiosity
h) practical

_____ 1. Edison asked questions constantly.
_____ 2. He worked on things that people wanted. He tried to make things that did not break easily, were easy to fix, and worked in ordinary conditions.
_____ 3. He organized the first industrial research lab. There, he directed teams of people in systematic research.
_____ 4. As a telegraph operator, Edison preferred the night shift because it gave him time for his experiments. He did not want an operation for his deafness. He said that silence helped his concentration.
_____ 5. He often did thousands of experiments to perfect an invention. For example, he did over 10,000 experiments to make a cheap battery for cars.
_____ 6. He went to school only three months.
_____ 7. Edison always worked very hard and seldom slept more than four hours a day.
_____ 8. He made over 1,000 inventions during his lifetime.

Activity G: Completing a paragraph

Put information about Edison into the framework below. Copy your paragraph on a clean sheet of paper. (NOTE: Most of the blanks require several words.)

Thomas Edison

Thomas Edison .... intensely curious and ....
constantly. He .... remarkable energy. He .... 4 hours a
day. He also .... remarkable determination. He ....
Edison .... a practical organizer who worked on .... and
organized the first .... He ....deaf, but did not want
.... deafness. He said .... concentration.

Activity H: Practicing for the dictation quiz on Form B

Study the structure and spelling in Form A. Make a cloze exercise with Form A. Omit every 3rd, 4th, or 5th word, as your teacher directs.

5.5 *TALENTED TWINS: Practice text*

Situation: Bill and Tom (p. 30) have twin friends named Lisa and Laura.

Activity A: Learning about Lisa and Laura

There are six pieces of information about Lisa and Laura in the box. Write one question about each piece of information. Work with a partner. Take turns asking and answering the questions.

1. When .... ?
2. Where .... ?
3. What .... ?
4. What .... ?
5. What .... like?
6. When .... ?

1. Date of birth: July, 1959
2. Place of birth: Albany, New York
3. Physical appearance:
   – hair: auburn
              wavy
   – eyes: hazel
              wideset
4. Personality and characteristics:
   – somewhat shy
   – dislike noisy parties
   – common sense
   – talented in music

5. Hobbies: all types of music
   ranging from classical to rock
   – Lisa: violin in the community
              orchestra
   – Laura: piano in a jazz group
6. Education
   – average students
   – major: English
   – degree: B.A. (1980)

Activity B: Making changes in paragraphs

Find the paragraph "Similar Siblings" in your notebook (see Activity A on page 30). Rewrite this paragraph with the information in the box. Change "Bill and Tom" to "Lisa and Laura." Use the title "Talented Twins."

5.6   *DESCRIBING APPEARANCE AND PERSONALITY: Spider diagram*

Activity A: Organizing vocabulary

These words answer the question, "What does s/he look like?" Put them in the spider diagram on page 94. You must sometimes decide whether a word applies only to men, only to women, or to both.

attractive	chubby	handsome	oval	slender
auburn	crooked	hazel	petite	slim
bald	curly	heavy	pimples (X)	stocky
bangs	dark (3)	long	pointed	straight
a beard	fair	a medium build	a ponytail	tall
beautiful	fat (X)	medium-height	pretty	thick
black (3)	freckles	medium-length	red	thin
blond	a good build	medium-weight	round	wavy
blue	a good figure	a moustache	salt-and-pepper	wide
braids	good-looking	muscular	short (2)	wide-set
brown (3)	gray	nice-looking	sideburns	wrinkles
a bun	green	ordinary-looking	skinny (X)	

(2) = use twice   (3) = use three times   (X) = impolite, even if true

Put a checkmark (√) beside thirteen nouns in the diagram that are used in this pattern: S/he has . . . .

»»→

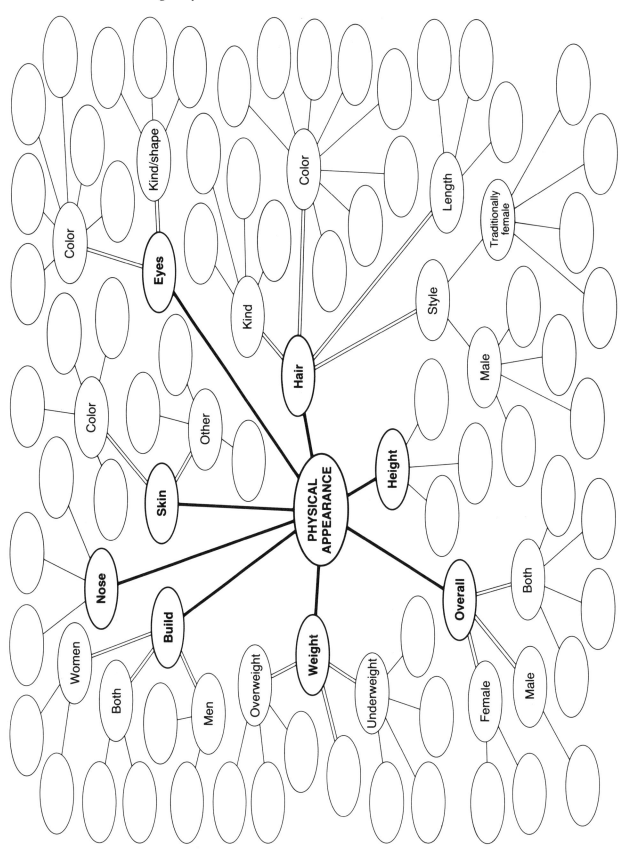

Activity B: Ordering adjectives in a series

You sometimes need two or three adjectives to describe someone's hair, eyes, beard, or other part of the body. Generally, you put the adjectives in this order:

S/he has (a/an) _____   _____   _____
                length/size   kind/shape   (shade) color

| |
| hair |
| eyes |
| eyebrows |
| eyelashes |
| beard |
| etc. |

Examples: She has short dark brown hair.
           He has a long bushy black beard.
           She has soft brown skin.

She has long hair. **NOT** *She has a long hair.*

Write each of the groups of words in the correct order on the corresponding blank lines. Add periods, question marks, and capital letters as needed.

1. round	2. he	3. black	4. nose	5. ponytails
has	eyebrows	have	auburn	medium-length
eyes	white	Tom	beard	twins
blue	does	Bill	big	dark
Betty	thick	eyelashes	grandpa	have
large	have	long	red	do
		and	a	blond
		curly	my	the
		both	an	
			and	
			has	

1. ....

....

2. ....

....

3. ....

....

4. ....

....

5. ....

....

⟫→

6. sideburns	7. father	8. braids	9. bangs	10. and
had	bald	your	a	grandmother
uncle	had	have	has	pointed
a	but	mother	Martha	had
thick	beard	did	long	hair
my	was	ever	and	a
black	short		bun	salt-and-pepper
moustache	my			my
gray	a			long
and	brown			nose

6. ....
....

7. ....
....

8. ....
....

9. ....
....

10. ....
....

Activity C: Matching opposites

These words are useful in answering the question, "What is s/he like?" Write each word in the list beside its opposite (antonym) in the box. Work with a partner or a small group. Match as many words as possible *before* using the dictionary.

cautious	immature	moody	serious
dishonest	impractical	not too bright	tactful
flexible	inconsiderate	optimistic	tolerant
grouchy	insecure	relaxed	undisciplined
hard-working	irresponsible	reserved	unselfish

blunt/ ....   lazy/ ....

cheerful/ ....   mature/ ....

confident/ ....   nervous/ ....

considerate/ ....   outgoing/ ....

critical/ ....   pessimistic/...........................

disciplined/ ....   practical/ ....

good-natured/ ....   responsible/ ....

honest/	selfish/ ....
impulsive/	stubborn/ ....
intelligent/	witty/ ....

5.7   REVISING: *Sylvia's self-portrait*

Sylvia wrote a paragraph about herself. She read it several times, but she wasn't happy with it. She rewrote it to make it better. Read her two paragraphs, and answer the questions.

1. How are the two paragraphs alike? ....

    ....

2. How are the paragraphs different? ....

    ....

3. Which paragraph is better? Why? ....

    ....

Box A

> ### Self-Portrait
>
> I am a practical, hard-working person. I am five feet seven inches tall and weigh 140 pounds. I have long wavy auburn hair. I sometimes have a ponytail, but only in the summer when I go swimming every day. I have light blue eyes, pale skin, and freckles. My nose is wide and flat. In general, I am an ordinary-looking person, except for my pretty hair.

Box B

> ### Self-Portrait
>
> I am a practical, hard-working person. I am five feet seven inches tall and weigh 140 pounds. My sister weighs 140 pounds, too. I have long wavy auburn hair. I sometimes have a ponytail, but only in the summer when I go swimming every day. Swimming is really fun. I have light blue eyes, pale skin, and freckles. In general, I am an ordinary-looking person, except for my pretty hair.

5.8 EDITING: Practice with symbols

Activity A: Finding editing problems

Cover the editing symbols. While you read the paragraph, put a checkmark (√) near each editing problem you find. Then uncover the symbols and compare them with your checks.

COVER↓

poss	My great-grandpa name was
ww	William Henry Langdon. Much people
VT	called him "Will," but I call him
	"Pappy." When he was in his twenties,
/	he had a curly brown hair, but by
ww, /	the age of 35 he had bald hair.
R(, Ⓥ∧	He was handsome and warm
WF, Ⓥ∧	blue eyes, he weight 200 lbs. and
⌐	tall 5 feet 9 inches. He was stocky
✗, Ⓢ∧	and very strong, because worked
	hard on his farm every day. Pappy
ⓐⁿᵗ∧	was practical man. He never bought
ww, VT	nothing that he does not need.
( )ᶠ, VT	Also generous man. He always give
	money and food to poor people.
	Unfortunately he also got angry
WF, WF	easy. Pappy liked hunt.
ᶠ(, rep	Because it was fun and it was
)ᶠ	practical.

Activity B: Making corrections

Rewrite the paragraph in Activity A. Make all necessary changes. Use the editing symbols and your checks as a guide.

5.9 DAN'S LEAST FAVORITE DAY: *Practice text*

Activity A: Combining sentences

Rewrite the paragraph. Combine the sentences as indicated. Use each of these words one time: *and*, *but*, *or*, *because*. Omit the numbers.

a) Combine 2 and 3.
b) Combine 5 and 6.
c) Combine 7 and 8.
d) Combine 9 and 10.

Dan's Least Favorite Day

[1]Dan hates to do his laundry. [2]He needs to wash his clothes every two weeks. [3]He always waits three weeks until everything is dirty. [4]He doesn't like to sort his clothes. [5]He usually forgets to take detergent to the laundromat. [6]He has to ask another customer for some of his. [7]He often has to get change in the grocery store. [8]The change machine in the laundromat seldom works. [9]He doesn't like to fold his clothes. [10]He doesn't like to put them on hangers. [11]In fact, Dan dislikes everything about doing his laundry with one exception. [12]He likes to finish! [13]That's why he always says, "When I'm rich, I will never do my own laundry again!"

Activity B: Making changes in paragraphs

1. Dan is rich now, so he never has to do his laundry. Now, he sends it out. Write about Dan before he became rich. Omit the numbers. Your first sentence: "Before Dan got rich, he hated to do his laundry."

2. Lisa and Laura dislike doing their laundry, too. Write about them. Omit the numbers. Your first sentence: "Lisa and Laura hate to do their laundry."

5.10 ACTIVE VOCABULARY PRACTICE: *Silent quizzes*

Your teacher will call out a number and demonstrate an action *silently*. Find the action on the list. Beside it, write the number the teacher called out.

Silent Quiz I

___ bite	___ clap	___ sneeze
___ blink	___ laugh	___ tiptoe
___ catch	___ point	___ try to reach
___ chew	___ smile	___ wave

Silent Quiz II

___ bend	___ cry	___ throw
___ blow	___ frown	___ wave
___ climb	___ kick	___ wink
___ cough	___ shrug	___ yawn

Silent Quiz III

___ ankle	___ fist	___ shoulder
___ cheeks	___ knee	___ toes
___ chin	___ neck	___ waist
___ elbow	___ shin	___ wrist

5.11 FAMILY HISTORY PROJECT – PERSONAL DESCRIPTION: Composition

Activity A: Describing personality

1. List six adjectives that describe the personality of your family member. Include both good and bad parts of his or her personality.

   a) ....

   b) ....

   c) ....

   d) ....

   e) ....

   f) ....

2. Take turns with a partner. Choose one adjective from your list, but keep your choice *secret*. Explain this word to your partner, but *don't* say the word on your list. Instead, illustrate the word by giving examples from your family member's life. Then show your list and ask your partner to identify the adjective you talked about.

   Example: a) lazy
               b) outgoing
               c) grouchy

   You say, "Her house was always full of people, especially on the weekends. She often invited friends or relatives to come for dinner and a game of cards."

Activity B: Describing interests

1. List six things your family member liked to do.

   a) ....

   b) ....

   c) ....

   d) ....

   e) ....

   f) ....

2. Choose two activities from your list. Explain what your family member regularly did that showed that she or he liked these activities. Write two sentences about each, but don't use the words from the list in your sentences.

   Example:

   Cooking
   She liked to prepare big, special meals for her family on all the holidays. Her kitchen was always full of homemade cookies for her visitors.

   1) ....

   ....

   ....

   ....

   2) ....

   ....

   ....

   ....

Activity C: Writing a description

Write a paragraph describing your family member. Tell about his or her personality, interests, and physical appearance. Use your ideas from Activities A and B as a starting point.

Unit 6   Describing People's Lives

(see Teacher's Manual pp. 41–49)

6.1   HALEY'S FAMILY HISTORY PROJECT: Dictation

Activity A: Dictation

Write the paragraph as your teacher dictates. When you finish, compare what you wrote with Form A in the box.

Haley's Family History Project (Form A)

As a child, Alex Haley, an American author, learned a few African words from his grandmother. They had been in his family for seven generations. These words helped Haley discover the tribal origin of his great-great-great-great-grandfather, Kunta Kinte. In 1767 Kinte was kidnapped in western Africa, brought to America, and sold as a slave. Eventually, Haley wrote <u>Roots</u>, a historical novel that tells Kinte's story and the next 200 years of Haley's family history.

Activity B: Talking about the dictation

Part I. Practice with information in the dictation.

1. What was in Haley's family for seven generations?
2. Who taught the words to Haley?
3. Who was Kunta Kinte?
4. How did Kunta Kinte become a slave?
5. What was the name of Haley's book?

Part II. Practice with information related to the dictation.

6. What is a root? Why did Haley use this word as the title for his book?
7. When did slavery end in the United States? Which U.S. president ended slavery?

Activity C: Making changes in paragraphs

Rewrite Form A. Substitute these words and phrases for other words with the same or similar meaning.

1. six-year-old
2. ancestor
3. shipped across the Atlantic
4. following
5. after twelve years of research and writing
6. used both facts and his own imagination to complete

Activity D: Adding information

Rewrite Form A. Add the following items in their logical places.

1. in chains
2. on her front porch in Tennessee
3. moving
4. black
5. along with court records, census lists, and maritime documents
6. The book, published in 1976, became a best seller and was soon made into a twelve-part television drama.

Activity E: Preparing for the dictation quiz on Form B

Study the words and structures in Form A. Make a cloze exercise by omitting every 3rd, 4th, or 5th word, as your teacher directs.

6.2   REVISING: "Edison's Most Famous Invention"

Activity A: Getting information from a lecture

Read these questions. Then listen as your teacher reads a short lecture about Thomas Edison's most famous invention. Take as many notes as you can, and use your notes to answer the questions.

1. What is Thomas Edison's most famous invention? ....
   ....
2. What does this invention do? ....
   ....
3. When did Edison begin working on it? ....
4. What was Edison's first problem? ....
   ....

5. What was his second problem? ....

....

6. What are the names of these parts of Edison's invention?

    a. ....

    b. ....

    c. ....

7. What was the total amount of time Edison worked on this invention? ....

....

8. How long did Edison's first bulb last? ....

   How long do modern ones last? ....

Edison with movie projector

Activity B: Working with a summary

In the box is Henry's first draft of a summary of the lecture about Edison's invention. Unfortunately, Henry didn't use his lecture notes while writing, so his summary has many factual mistakes and missing words. Read Henry's summary and help him begin to revise it.

1. Check the facts in the summary. Use your lecture notes from Activity A. Find and circle 15 FACTUAL mistakes in the summary.
2. Fill in the blanks in the summary with these words:

oxygen	filament	glows	electricity	carbonized thread
vacuum	melt	practical	through	bamboo

Henry's summary

Edison's Least Famous Invention

1   Edison's most famous invention is the electric light bulb. Edison began to

2   work on it in 1879 and did a few experiments during two years. His plan was to

3   change _____ into light by passing an electric

4   current through a thin piece of material. When electricity passes _____

5   a material, the material gets very cold. When this happens, the material

6   _____ brightly and makes light.

7   His first problem was _____ . When

8   it is present, materials burn easily. There is oxygen in air, so Edison

9   needed to keep water away from his materials. He made a metal bulb and

10   put his materials inside it. Then he took the air out of the bulb and made a

11   _____ inside it.

12   Edison's second and more difficult problem was to find the best material

13   for the _____ . He needed something that did not _____ ,

14   that glowed brightly, and that lasted a short time. He tried a few materials. He

15   even used a blond hair from a friend's beard. It worked well. He also used

16   platinum. The platinum filament worked, but not well, and it was very

17   inexpensive. Finally, he used a _____ . His filament of

18   carbonized thread worked! It was cheap and had a high melting point. Thus, in

19   1879, the first _____ electric light bulb was born. A year later,

20   with a filament of carbonized _____ , it was ready to sell.

21   Modern light bulbs are the same as Edison's first bulb. His lasted for only

22   four hours, but today's bulbs have an average life of more than 1,000 years.

23   Also, his bulb had a vacuum inside, but modern bulbs are filled with nitrogen

24   and oxygen.

Activity C: Revising the summary

On a clean sheet of paper, revise Henry's summary by recopying it and correcting the 15 factual mistakes you circled. Use your lecture notes from Activity A to make the corrections.

6.3   *WORKING WITH A BIOGRAPHY:*   *Edison*

Activity A: Collecting biographical information

A biography is the story of a person's life. Look at your papers about Thomas Edison from this unit and Units 3 and 5 to find information about his life. Work with a partner or small group to complete the outline.

Facts about Edison's Life

A. *Childhood*
  1. Birth – Ohio – Feb. 11, ___?___
  2. Loved ___?___ – very good memory – ___?___ about science
  3. ___?___ mos. of formal educ. – trouble in school – mother became teacher

B. *Adolescence*
  1. 1859 – 1st job – selling newspapers + snacks on trains – accident made him ___?___
  2. printed own newspaper + had lab in baggage car – result: started fire + lost job
  3. 1862 – telegraph operator on night shift – made an invention to do his work – result: fired for sleeping

C. *Important events in career*
  1. 1869 – 1st patented invention – not wanted – result: worked on what people ___?___
  2. 1870 – 1st sale – stock price printer – $40,000 – result: opened lab + factory – Newark, New Jersey
  3. 1876 – world's 1st industrial ___?___ lab – Menlo Park, N.J. – teams of people – systematic research – 40 inventions at once – this organization perhaps = greatest invention

>>>→

D. Important inventions
  1. Many inventions, # = ? _____ ; examples: ? _____ ,
     motion-picture camera, cheap storage ? _____ for cars +
     streetcars
  2. improvements on telephone + telegraph
  3. most famous invention = 1st practical electric light ? _____
     in ? _____ ; filament = ? _____ thread – tested many
     materials, # = ? _____ – more than 1 year later : ready
     for sale

E. Personal data
  1. married twice – 5 children – son, Gov. of N.J.
  2. refused operation for ? _____ – said silence helped
     ? _____
  3. unusual daily routine – ? _____ hrs. of sleep per day
  4. genius = ? _____ % perspiration + ? _____ % inspiration
  5. death – Oct. 17, ? _____ – still working

Activity B: Completing a short biography

1. Compare the outline in Activity A with the biography of Edison.

   a) How many divisions are in the outline?
   b) How many paragraphs are in the biography?
   c) What is the topic of each paragraph?

2. Fill in the blanks in the biography of Edison. Use facts from the outline and
   your knowledge of English. Work with a partner or small group.

Edison: America's Most Famous _____

1   Thomas _____ Edison was born _____ Ohio _____

2   February 11, 1847. He loved books, had _____ excellent memory, and

3   showed curiosity about science, _____ he had trouble in school. After

4   only three months of formal _____ , he left school and

5   _____ at home with his mother.

6   When Edison was only _____ years old, he began working.

7   First, he _____ newspapers and snacks on trains. One day, someone

8   grabbed his ears to pull him on a moving train, and he became almost

9   _____. Later, he printed his own newspaper and _____

10   experiments in the baggage car of a train. He lost this job _____

11   an experiment started a fire on the train. Next, at the age of _____ ,

12   Edison worked as a telegraph operator. He _____

13   the night shift because he had time for his experiments. He lost this job

14   _____ he was _____ while a new invention

15   did his work.

16   _____ 1869, Edison got his _____ patent on an invention, but

17   no one wanted it. After _____ , he worked on things people wanted.

18   In 1870, he finally _____ an invention for $40,000. He immediately

19   used this _____ to open a lab and factory in Newark, New Jersey.

20   _____ years later, in Menlo Park, _____ _____ ,

21   Edison opened the world's first _____ research lab.

22   There, he directed teams of people in systematic research on 40 inventions

23   at _____ time. Today some people think this organization was Edison's

24   _____ invention.

25   During his _____ Edison made more than _____

26   inventions, including the _____ , the motion-picture

27   camera, and a cheap storage battery _____ automobiles and streetcars.

28   He also _____ the telephone and telegraph. But his most

29   famous invention changed _____ into light. He

30   experimented with thousands of materials. In _____ , he passed an

31   electric current through a _____ of carbonized thread and

32   the first _____ electric light bulb was born. After

33   one more _____ of work, it was finally ready to sell.

34   Edison had a remarkable life. He married _____ times, and one

35   of his five children became Governor of New Jersey. Edison never had an

36   operation for his _____ . He _____ that silence

37   helped his concentration. He always worked very hard and _____

38   slept more than _____ hours a day. He believed that _____

39   was 99% perspiration and 1% inspiration. He was probably right. His eighty-

40   four _____ of energy and creativity changed the world. When he

41   _____ on October 17, _____ , he was still _____

42   on new ideas.

6.4   PERSONALITY PROFILE: *Composition/newspaper activity*

Activity A: Preparing questions for an interview

Here are some questions you can ask when you interview people about their lives. Complete the questions by filling in the blanks.

Childhood

1. What .... full name?

2. When and where .... born?

3. What .... | mother |
   | father | do?

4. How many brothers and sisters .... have?

   .... the oldest, the youngest, in the middle?

5. Where .... grow up?

6. What .... interested in when ....
   a child?

Education

7. | Where |
   | When | .... go to high school?

8. | Where |
   | When | .... college as
   an undergraduate?

   What .... major?

   When .... graduate?

9. | Where |
   | When | .... go to graduate school?

   In what field .... do your graduate work?

   What degree did you............?

Career

10. What jobs .... had and when?

11. What .... present job?

    How long .... had it?

12. What .... like about your present job?

    What .... dislike about it?

13. Why .... choose this career?

14. What .... professional goals for the future?

Personal information

15. How long .... lived here?

    .... lived in another country?

16. .... married?

    (.............. .... children?)

17. What .... like to do in your leisure time?

18. What .... like best about yourself?

    What .... like to change about yourself?

19. In general, what .... your philosophy of life?

20. What .... your personal goals for the future?

Activity B: Practicing with the questions

Do a practice interview. Ask your teacher the questions you prepared in Activity A. Take careful notes of the answers.

Activity C: Interviewing a visitor

Your teacher will invite a visitor to your class. Use the questions from Activity A to interview this visitor. Take turns asking questions. Take careful notes of the answers. Use the notes to write a "Personality Profile" article for the class newspaper.

6.5 PROFESSIONAL PROFILE: Practice text

Activity A: Adding verbs

Fill in the blanks with the correct tenses of the verbs in this list. Use each verb at least one time.

attend	earn	have
be	enjoy	intend
become	enter	work

Situation: During Career Week, students at Midburg High School did interviews for a project called "Professional Profiles." Here is one of their reports.

Professional Profile: Charlotte Kyler

Charlotte Kyler (1) .... over twenty-two years of experience in banking. She (2)....................... currently a loan officer at the Midburg National Bank where she (3) .... for seventeen years. Ms. Kyler (4) .... interested in a banking career at the age of sixteen while she (5) .... part-time in a bank during her summer vacation. She (6) .... Middle State University and (7) .... both graduate and undergraduate degrees in finance. Her first job (8) .... at Community State Bank where she (9) .... for five years. Ms. Kyler (10) .... on the city council since 1982 and (11).................... to run for mayor in the next election. In her leisure time she (12)....................... jogging and hiking and often (13)....................... local races. A native of Faraway, Montana, Ms. Kyler (14)....................... married to architect Cranston Davis. They (15)............................. two sons, who (16)................................. Middle State University.

Activity B: Making changes in paragraphs

Unfortunately, Charlotte Kyler died in a car accident two days after the interview. Rewrite the paragraph with the necessary changes. Begin with "The late Charlotte Kyler...."

6.6 *ACTIVE VOCABULARY PRACTICE:* *Verb review*

Directions: Choose items from the list to complete the answers to the questions below. In Exercises A and B together, you can use every item at least one time. (Some questions have more than one answer.)

blink	kick	snap my fingers
blow a bubble	laugh	sneeze
bite my nails	make a fist	throw
catch	point	tickle his/her ribs
clap	raise my hand	tiptoe
cough	rub on lotion	whisper
cry	scratch	whistle
dial	shake hands	wink
draw a heart	shrug my shoulders	yawn
frown	slap it	

Exercise A

1. . . . you have a cold

2. . . . you are sleepy

3. . . . a mosquito bites you

4. . . . you are going to spend all day at the beach

5. . . . you want to ask a question in class

6. . . . you don't know an answer

7. . . . the baby is sleeping

8. . . . the sun is in your eyes

9. . . . you hear something funny

10. . . . you liked the concert

11. . . . you are nervous

12. . . . you are teasing

1 . . . .

2 . . . .

3 . . . .

4 . . . .

5 . . . .

6 . . . .

7 . . . .

8 . . . .

9 . . . .

10 . . . .

11 . . . .

12 . . . .

Exercise B

1. . . . you are angry

2. . . . you are unhappy

1 . . . .

2 . . . .

⋙→

3. . . . you want to tell a secret

3 ....

4. . . . you play soccer

4 ....

5. . . . you play baseball

5 ....

6. . . . you meet someone for the first time

6 ....

7. . . . you are chewing bubble gum

7 ....

8. . . . you give directions

8 ....

9. . . . you are keeping time with the music

9 ....

10. . . . you want to make someone laugh

10 ....

11. . . . you are making a phone call

11 ....

12. . . . you are making a valentine

12 ....

6.7　FAMILY HISTORY PROJECT – SIGNIFICANT EVENT: Composition

Activity A: Talking about a significant event

1. Choose one important event from your family member's life.

2. Work with a partner. Tell your partner about the significant event you chose. Make sure your partner can answer these questions:

   – What year did the event happen?
   – Where did it happen?
   – How old was your family member then?
   – What happened?
   – Why was this event significant in the person's life?

Activity B: Writing and reading about the event

1. Write about the significant event. Use the past tense. Make sure your paper answers the questions in Activity A.

2. Exchange papers with the same partner that you talked to in Activity A. Read your partner's paper. Tell your partner about anything that is not clear. Also, tell your partner about any additions that are needed.

3. Rewrite your paper. Make the changes and additions that your partner suggested.

Activity C: Editing papers

1. Read your partner's paper carefully. Underline all the verbs.

2. Reread the paper. Look for verb problems. Circle any verbs that are incorrect in any way. Remember that the event took place in the *past*.

3. Explain to your partner all the problems in his or her paper that you find.

4. Rewrite your own paper. Correct all types of problems you and your partner found. Make sure to correct all verb problems.

6.8   FAMILY HISTORY PROJECT – SHORT BIOGRAPHY: Composition

Activity A: Making an outline for a biography

Work with a partner or small group. Put each piece of information in this list under one of the four headings in the box. Then put the items under each heading in a logical order. Copy the finished outline on a clean sheet of paper.

> A. Childhood and early years
> B. Adulthood
> C. Older years
> D. Personal information

activities as a teenager
childhood interests
community service activities
date & place of birth
date of marriage; spouse's name; ages at marriage
date, place, & cause of death
education outside school
first job
health; health problems
hometown as an adult
hometown as a child
important event(s) in later years
languages and travel
lifelong interests
military service
# of brothers & sisters; order of birth
# of sons & daughters
# of years of education; graduation & major
   occupation(s); events in career
parents' names, occupations & economic status
personality traits (strengths & weaknesses)
philosophy of life; famous quotations
physical appearance as a young adult
religion
residence during older years
retirement date & activities
significant event(s) during adulthood
significant event(s) during childhood

Activity B: Outlining your family member's life

Begin with the outline from Activity A. Add, omit, or change the place or order of information to fit your family member's life. Beside each item in this new outline, write specific facts about your family member. Use information from your "Family History Fact Sheet" on page 42. (NOTE: "Facts about Edison's Life" on pages 107–8 is an example of how your finished outline will look.)

Activity C: Writing a biography

Write a short biography of your family member. Use the outline you made in Activity B as a guide.

6.9 *FAMILY HISTORY PROJECT – FINAL PAPER:* Composition

Activity A: Reviewing your papers

In addition to the short biography, you have five other papers about your family member. Find and reread these papers:

a) first thoughts   d) a personal description
b) typical daily routine   e) a significant event
c) an important place

Activity B: Organizing the parts

1. To finish your family history project, you will integrate your shorter papers with the biography to make *one* longer final paper for your future reader. Here is a diagram of the basic organization of the final paper, and one person's plan for integrating all of his papers.

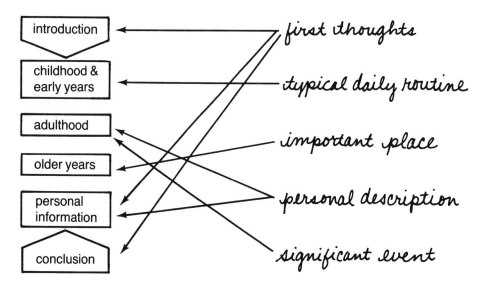

2. On a clean sheet of paper, draw a diagram of the basic organization of the final paper and *your* plan of integration.

Activity C: Writing the final paper

Write your final paper. Follow the plan you drew in Activity B.

Appendixes

Appendix 1: Creating a Class Newspaper

MAKING OVERALL PLANS

Glance at the two pages from a sample class newspaper on pages 122–23. Then quickly flip through *all* the newspaper activities in the book to get a sense of the whole project. *Your* calendar of events, rather than the sequence of units in the book, may determine the best time for scheduling some of them. In particular, you will need to make arrangements for the class trip (Unit 4), the survey about the typical student (Unit 5), and the personality profile interview (Unit 6). These activities, which put students in contact with people from outside the class, generate considerable student interest and are well worth a little advance planning. Also, decide when you want to "publish" the newspaper. You may want to do two or three small issues or one elaborate one. Set deadlines accordingly.

CHOOSING A FORMAT

Individual copies   How you "publish" your class newspaper depends on facilities and circumstances. If at all possible, arrange to make a copy for each student in the class and enough extras for the students' other teachers and school administrators. Photocopying the paper is easier than duplicating it by ditto or mimeo. If your school cannot afford the photocopying, perhaps the students can pay for their own copies.

Single display copy   If you cannot make individual copies, make one copy and display it prominently, just as in earlier times newspapers were posted for everyone to pass by and read. Either type the display newspaper or make a more readable display by making a "giant" newspaper with articles, headlines, and graphics handwritten by students. Have an "unveiling ceremony" at the publication reception described on page 121.

LAYING OUT THE NEWSPAPER

Basic procedure   The basic procedure is simple. Type or write the articles in columns. Cut out the columns, arrange them attractively on pages (or posterboard), and stick them down. Write in headlines, and fill in the blank spaces with drawings, graphs, cartoons, acknowledgments, and "ads." When laying out the front page, attach columns to one of the student-designed masthead pages from Activity E in section 1.10.

Student participation   Enlist as much student help as possible in the layout process, either before, during, or after class. Also, include as many different individuals as possible. Any one student should not work on everything because the finished newspaper should have some surprises to make it more interesting to read. Emphasize participation rather than perfection. The layout is rich with opportunities to give less talented language learners a sense of positive personal involvement in something associated with their English class.

Preliminary layout   If time permits, devote a class session to preliminary layout. First, look at commercial papers and newsletters. Talk about where different types of articles go in a paper and what makes a page attractive. Then put students to work with scissors, rulers, pencils, small markers, tape, blank paper, copies of articles typed in columns *without* headlines (one set of articles for each pair of students), and a list of headlines. If some students are floundering, help them decide what will go on each page, but not in what arrangement. Try to leave them with enough freedom to develop their own ideas. Collect the students' papers for ideas and artwork to use in the final layout.

Final layout   If you don't have class time for preliminary layouts, arrange the articles and attach them to pages. Take the pages to class, and have a variety of students print in the headlines and page headings, and add the artwork. In making the final layout, you can use ordinary cellophane tape, even masking tape, or almost any kind of paste or glue; however, double-stick tape and/or a glue stick are more convenient to use.

Double-sided layout   Lay out the newspaper to be printed on both sides of the page if you can. Such an arrangement looks more authentic and allows double-page spreads. If double-sided copying is not feasible, you can achieve a double-sided effect. Just have students staple or tape pages together with blank sides back to back before they staple the whole paper together.

PREPARING ARTICLES FOR LAYOUT

Typing   Try to get selections in final form as you go to avoid a last-minute rush. Type them in columns as soon as you can. If possible, have students type and proofread them. Take a portable typewriter to be used in a corner somewhere. Or, arrange for student access to a machine already on the premises.

Column size   When typing selections for layout, set the margins to make columns 3½ inches wide, and use a guide sheet. To make one, just take a clean sheet of typing paper and draw two heavy vertical lines 3½ inches apart with a dark marker. Put the guide sheet into the machine behind the page you are typing, and keep your typing between the lines.

Cloze format   Type at least one selection per issue with blanks every 7th word or so. In this format the selection serves as a cloze exercise in the class session devoted to reading the paper. Particularly good choices for this treatment are articles that all of the students have worked on.

Headlines   Have students write headlines as the articles are produced. Start by giving students several headlines to choose from. Discuss why some are better than others. Build to students' writing headlines themselves if possible.

MAKING ILLUSTRATIONS

Drawings   Since the class newspaper is by and for the students, drawings made by students of themselves and other classmates are easy and appropriate decorations. As a quick exercise in following directions, similar to Active Vocabulary Practice, ask students to draw two squares, each approximately one inch by one inch. In one square have them draw their own faces, and in the other square the face of a student of the opposite sex. During this activity, chuckles and interaction among the students are guaranteed. Collect the

drawings, and use them to decorate "Meet the Class" or "In Search of the Typical Student." Or, use them as borders or as fillers throughout the paper.

Advertisements   "Ads" stimulate creativity and fun. Have students design advertisements to promote travel to their cities or countries. Or, specify ads for instant and preposterous study aids such as TOEFL pills, grammar injections, and perfect-English pencils.

⟫→

Cartoons   To make cartoons, show students a few examples of cartoons and comics from newspapers and magazines. Then display some frames from which you have deleted the captions, and have students write their own captions. Discuss aspects of the students' common situation that might serve as inspiration for cartoons. List the ideas generated, and have artistic students develop the pictures.

Graphs   Graphs are great for bringing math, geography, etc., into the English class. Show examples of different kinds of graphs from newspapers, magazines, or textbooks. Copy (or have a student copy) one or two simple graphs on a transparency or big paper. Prepare questions, true-false statements, and/or fill-ins over these samples. Finally, have one to three interested students make their own graphs. Nationalities of students in the English program or their native languages are possible topics.

EXPANDING THE CONTENTS OF THE NEWSPAPER

Interviews   Have students interview other students in the school who have participated in events, trips, or homestays arranged by the English program. If you are teaching in a non-English-speaking country and some students have visited English-speaking countries, have student "reporters" interview the "travelers" for reports on their visits.

Reports on school events   Have students collect information and write reports on upcoming or past English-program or school events.

Horoscope   Create a feature called "Your Ideal Horoscope." First, have students read horoscopes taken from commercial newspapers and magazines and answer questions about them. If possible, also record a telephone horoscope and bring it to class for transcription or listening cloze. Then ask students to write "ideal" predictions and advice for their individual astrological signs. In other words, have them write what they would like to read (predictions) or what they need to read (advice). Compile the predictions and advice into the form of a horoscope for publication.

Advice column   (1) Select two or three advice columns from commercial newspapers and magazines, and condense each problem letter into a single question. Then ask students to read the columns, determine which letters state problems and which letters give advice, and match the condensations with the problem letters. (2) Have students work in small groups or pairs to write their own problem letters. Suggest that they write about typical problems of students or use their humor and imagination to invent problems. (3) Make a handout of two to five letters based on or chosen from the problem letters the students wrote. Have students write advice letters in reply. (4) Compile the students' problem letters and advice letters into a column for publication. Whenever necessary, combine similar letters or pad skimpy letters. Have students choose a name for their advice column and draw a picture of the adviser.

Potpourri   Have students write articles on one or more of these topics: recipes/descriptions of typical meals and dishes from students' countries; reviews of restaurants that serve the students' native foods; restaurant/food opinion poll in which students interview teachers and others about their favorite restaurants or recipes; and reviews or polls about current or all-time movie, book, or record favorites or worsts.

PUBLISHING AND READING THE NEWSPAPER

In-class activities   Give students some time to look over the whole issue silently. Then ask questions based on information scattered throughout the issue. Have students respond to each question by giving only the number of the page and headline of the article where they would *look for* the the answer. Hand out a list of the *same* questions with a space for each answer and its page number. See who can find all of the information first. Next, have students write two to four questions of their own, each on a slip of paper. Ask students to put their names on the strips too. Make two teams, and draw the students' questions from a bag. Read the questions, and give points for correct answers. Read any malformed questions correctly without mentioning that there was any error. Finally, do the cloze exercise if you have used such a format in typing up one of the articles. Work the crossword puzzle, and enjoy your collective accomplishment.

Publication reception   When the newspaper is finished, organize a reception for at least two or three guests. Send invitations, written of course, to another class, the director, the school secretary, and/or other sympathetic people. Plan and rehearse a short program with a student acting as the master of ceremonies, and other students presenting/ reading each newspaper selection. If possible, snap a few photos and close with simple refreshments.

≫→

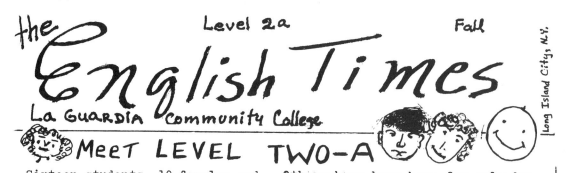

the English Times
Level 2a   Fall
La Guardia Community College
Long Island City, N.Y.

Meet LEVEL TWO-A

Sixteen students, 10 females and 6 males, ___ in the level-2A class at LaGuardia Community College. They _____ from 8 countries in ____, Africa, America, and Europe. They _____ the following native languages: Arabic, Chinese, Greek, Korean, Spanish, and Tigre. In _____ countries they had various occupations. Twelve of them ___ students. Other occupations included beautician, electrical technician, and driver.

The students _____ in age from 20 to 41 years. The _____ age is 28.7 years. One student has been in the U.S. ____ 9½ years.

Others have been here for only two months. The _____ length of time in the U.S. is 3.75 years.

Six of the students ____ married. Only three students _____ alone. The others live with their spouses and/or relatives.

_____ teachers work with the level-2A class: Drena Contreras, Beverly Ingram, and Susan _____. According to these teachers, the class, on the whole, _____ hard and cooperates well. The teachers _____, " It is really a pleasure to work with such a lovely group of people."

LEVEL TWO VISITS ZOO

Eleven level-two _____ from La Guardia College _____ to the Bronx Zoo on May 22. About 9:45 a.m. Tracey and the students _____ La Guardia and _____ at the zoo about 11 a.m. It _____ a long time to arrive at the zoo _____ the group started late from school, and the zoo was far. Beverly and _____ son, Kevin, _____ waiting at the zoo entrance. Kids were everywhere because _____ is free on Tuesdays. Nicolas and Nader arrived later, just before lunch, because they had trouble with the _____. They found the group because they saw Tracey on a bench near the cable _____.

In the morning the students walked around the zoo in small groups, took photos, and looked _____ the animals. The group _____

Cont. pg. 2*

An Important Essay

Two weeks ago I went to 34th St. to a big store to buy a wool skirt for winter. I had three or four hundred dollars in my handbag. While I was waiting at the cashier to buy the skirt, I didn't find the money. My handbag was open. The money was gone. I felt afraid. I didn't buy the skirt.

Before this experience took place in my life, I wasn't nervous. I'm very careful now. I carry my handbag in front of me, not behind. This day was very instructive for me.   -Aouatif Zerrad-Hyalouki-

TODAY'S WEATHER

Clear, sunny skies, day time high: 75°F, low tonight: 60°F

P.S To enjoy today's weather go to El Valle, Colombia, in June.

Reporter: Edilma Torres

Answers to "What's My City?"
4.A, 7.B, 2.C, 5.D, 1.E, 6.F, 3.G.

*Page 2 is not shown here.

WHAT'S MY CITY ?

3

Reporters: Jose Cardenas, Jorge Castro, Nuo Cen, Michael Damianou, Chong Hak Kong, Ethel Osorio, Juan Carlos Prieto

Test your knowledge of travel and geography. Match the city and its description. Put the numbers in the blanks below. Good luck! (Check your answers on page **1** .)

1. Canton (China)
2. Choulou (Cyprus)
3. Estepona (Spain)
4. Inchon (Korea)
5. Medellin (Colombia)
6. Palmira (Colombia)
7. Santa Marta (Colombia)

____ A. It takes 50 minutes by train to go from my city to the capital. The principal product is salt.

____ B. My city is small, but very beautiful because of the beach. It is one of my country's most important seaports on the Atlantic Ocean.

____ C. Five hundred people live in my town. The land there is hilly and good for farming.

____ D. My city is situated between mountains in a valley crossed by a medium river. Its botanical gardens, especially the orchids, are famous.

____ E. My city has a long history. It has many famous universities and buildings. It also has many, many food factories. In the spring the ground is full of flowers, My city's other name is "flower city."

____ F. My city is in a valley in the south of my country. The principal industry is sugar cane and other agriculture.

____ G. My city is called "the sun of the coast." The principal industry is tourism. All of the city is interesting because of the Arabic architecture.

The Tank was Empty

Six years ago I lived in Athens. Every fifteen days I went to my village with my friend who had a new Italian car. One Friday the engine didn't work. My friend got out of his car and looked at it. He didn't see anything. For one hour he and I looked everywhere. We checked everything. Finally, after one hour we looked in the gas tank. It didn't have any gasoline! My friend and I felt terrible because the day before he had filled the tank, and today, it didn't have any gasoline. Anyway, together we put gasoline in the tank and went to my village. In the end my friend was lucky because the thief took only the gasoline. He still has his car.
                    -John Lapatsanis-

the Robbery

Last month I went shopping and saw a robbery. I saw it because I was inside shopping. A bad man took a lot of jewelry and stole other things. It was important to me because I saw a bad thing done. A policeman saw the bad man and stopped him. I was very sad because it was real, and it wasn't good.   -Ana Clara Restrepo-

An Afraid Night

When I had just come to New York, I was not afraid when I walked home at night. One thing happened to my good friend to change me. One night, my good friend was going home after work. She was walking on the sidewalk. There were no people or cars in the street. Suddenly, a tall man jumped out of a doorway to come near her. He pulled out a sharp knife. He took her new handbag and expensive watch. He left. My friend did not say anything because she was very afraid. She lost a watch that cost $200 and $50 in money. After that, my friend didn't walk on the sidewalk at night. She bought a car to drive home. When my friend told me this dangerous thing, I was very afraid. Now I don't walk home at night. I'm very careful at night.   -Xiao-He Zhao-

ENGLISH TIMES

Fall
Level 2a

Appendix 2: Editing Symbols

Symbols for mistakes in grammar and mechanics

Symbol	Explanation	Sentence marked with symbols	Corrected sentence
1. (sp)	spelling error	Bev and Carol are teechers. *(sp)*	Bev and Carol are teachers.
2. ‿	Connect and make one word.	They like to work to‿gether.	They like to work together.
3. ⌄	Add something.	They ⌄ born in Texas. *(were)*	They were born in Texas.
4. /	Omit this.	They are / good friends.	They are good friends.
5. ww	wrong word	Carol lives at Austin, Texas. *ww*	Carol lives in Austin, Texas.
6. wf	right word, wrong form	Both of them enjoy teach. *wf*	Both of them enjoy teaching.
7. #	number error, singular↔plural	They met fifteen year ago. *#*	They met fifteen years ago.
8. poss	Use possessive form.	Bev home is now in New York City. *poss*	Bev's home is now in New York City.
9. vt	verb tense error	Carol work in Malaysia in 1986. *vt*	Carol worked in Malaysia in 1986.
10. sv agr	subject-verb agreement error	Bev have two sons. *sv agr*	Bev has two sons.
11. pro agr	pronoun agreement error	Carol always enjoys himself at parties. *pro agr*	Carol always enjoys herself at parties.
12. rep	repetition	Every day Carol has coffee daily. *rep*	Every day Carol has coffee.
13. ⌐	word order error	They taught in Algeria English.	They taught English in Algeria.
14. c, ¢	capitalization error	both of them like Languages. *c* *¢*	Both of them like languages.
15. P, P̸	punctuation error	They both, speak French	They both speak French.

16. ( )^R	run-on sentence	(Bev taught in Mexico, it was great.)^R	Bev taught in Mexico. It was great.
17. ( )^F	fragment error	(After they taught French.)^F	After college they taught French.
18. ¶, ⫯	paragraph error		

Symbols for types of words

19. S	subject	⑤ ‸Worked in Tunisia.	Carol worked in Tunisia.
20. V	verb	Ⓥ Carol ‸also a lawyer.	Carol is also a lawyer.
21. aux	auxiliary verb	ⓐⓤⓧ Where ‸Bev learn Spanish?	Where did Bev learn Spanish?
22. pron	pronoun	ⓟⓡⓞⓝ Bev loves ‸husband very much.	Bev loves her husband very much.
23. prep	preposition	ⓟⓡⓔⓟ In 1983 they went ‸Toronto.	In 1983 they went to Toronto.
24. art	article	ⓐⓡⓣ Bev wants to take ‸trip to Brazil.	Bev wants to take a trip to Brazil.
25. adj	adjective	Carol and Bev wrote a ⓦⓕ, ⓤⓢⓔ ⓐⓓⓙ wonderfully book.	Carol and Bev wrote a wonderful book.
26. adv	adverb	Carol and Bev make friends ⓦⓕ, ⓤⓢⓔ ⓐⓓⓥ quick.	Carol and Bev make friends quickly.
27. conj	conjunction	Both of them like Chinese, ⓒⓞⓝⓙ Japanese, ‸Thai food.	Both of them like Chinese, Japanese, and Thai food.

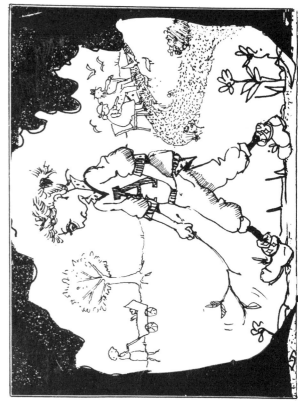